BOB DOLE

GREAT ACHIEVERS

LIVES OF THE PHYSICALLY CHALLENGED

BOB DOLE

POLITICIAN

Marcia Wertime

Chelsea House Publishers

Philadelphia

CHELSEA HOUSE PUBLISHERS

EDITORIAL DIRECTOR   Richard Rennert
EXECUTIVE MANAGING EDITOR   Karyn Gullen Browne
COPY CHIEF   Robin James
PICTURE EDITOR   Adrian G. Allen
CREATIVE DIRECTOR   Robert Mitchell
ART DIRECTOR   Joan Ferrigno
PRODUCTION MANAGER   Sallye Scott

GREAT ACHIEVERS: LIVES OF THE PHYSICALLY CHALLENGED

SENIOR EDITOR   Kathy Kuhtz Campbell
SERIES DESIGN   Basia Niemczyc

Staff for **BOB DOLE**
EDITORIAL ASSISTANT   Scott D. Briggs
PICTURE RESEARCHER   Matthew Dudley
COVER ILLUSTRATION   Bill Farnsworth

First Printing

1 3 5 7 9 8 6 4 2

Library of Congress Cataloging-in-Publication Data

Wertime, Marcia.
Bob Dole: politician / Marcia Wertime.
p. cm.—(Great achievers)
Includes bibliographical references and index.
Summary: Relates the story of a soldier from Russell, Kansas, who was injured in
World War II and who went on to become a Republican senator in the United States
Congress.
ISBN 0-7910-2084-3.
     0-7910-2097-5 (pbk.)
1. Dole, Robert J., 1923– —Juvenile literature. 2. Legislators—United States—
Biography—Juvenile literature. 3. Unites States—Congress—Senate—Biog-
raphy—Juvenile literature. [1. Dole, Robert J., 1923– 2. Legislators.] I. Title.
II. Series: Great achievers (Chelsea House Publishers)
E840.8.D64D65 1996   95-18489
328.73'092—dc20   CIP
[B]   AC

FRONTISPIECE:

*While campaigning for the Republican nomination for president in
January 1988, Senator Bob Dole of Kansas speaks to the press during
a news conference in Chicago, Illinois.*

CONTENTS

GREAT ACHIEVERS

LIVES OF THE PHYSICALLY CHALLENGED

JIM ABBOTT
baseball star

LUDWIG VAN BEETHOVEN
composer

LOUIS BRAILLE
inventor

CHRIS BURKE
actor

ROY CAMPANELLA
baseball star

RAY CHARLES
musician

BOB DOLE
politician

STEPHEN HAWKING
physicist

ERNEST HEMINGWAY
writer

JACKIE JOYNER-KERSEE
champion athlete

HELEN KELLER
humanitarian

RON KOVIC
antiwar activist

MARIO LEMIEUX
ice hockey star

MARLEE MATLIN
actress

MARY TYLER MOORE
actress

FLANNERY O'CONNOR
author

ITZHAK PERLMAN
violinist

FRANKLIN D. ROOSEVELT
U.S. president

HENRI DE TOULOUSE-LAUTREC
artist

VINCENT VAN GOGH
artist

STEVIE WONDER
musician

A Message for Everyone

Jerry Lewis

Close to half a century ago—when I was the ripe old age of 23—an incredible stroke of fate rocketed me to overnight stardom as an entertainer. After the initial shock wore off, I began to have a very strong feeling that, in return for all life had given me, I must find a way of giving something back. At just that moment, a deeply moving experience in my personal life persuaded me to take up the leadership of a fledgling battle to defeat a then little-known group of diseases called muscular dystrophy, as well as other related neuromuscular diseases—all of which are disabling and, in the worst cases, cut life short.

In 1950, when the Muscular Dystrophy Association (MDA)—of which I am national chairman—was established, physical disability was looked on as a matter of shame. Franklin Roosevelt, who guided America through World War II from a wheelchair, and Harold Russell, the World War II hero who lost both hands in battle, then became an Academy Award–winning movie star and chairman of the President's Committee on Employment of the Handicapped, were the exceptions. One of the reasons that muscular dystrophy and related diseases were so little known was that people who had been disabled by them were hidden at home, away from the pity and discomfort with which they were generally regarded by society. As I got to know and began working with people who have disabilities, I quickly learned what a tragic mistake this perception was. And my determination to correct this terrible problem soon became as great as my commitment to see disabling neuromuscular diseases wiped from the face of the earth.

I have long wondered why it never occurs to us, as we experience the knee-jerk inclination to feel sorry for people who are physically disabled, that lives such as those led by President Roosevelt, Harold Russell, and all of the extraordinary people profiled in this Great Achievers series demonstrate unmistakably how wrong we are. Physical disability need not be something that blights life and destroys opportunity for personal fulfillment and accomplishment. On the contrary, as people such as Ray Charles, Stephen Hawking, and Ron Kovic prove, physical disability can be a spur to greatness rather than a condemnation of emptiness.

In fact, if my experience with physically disabled people can be taken as a guide, as far as accomplishment is concerned, they have a slight edge on the rest of us. The unusual challenges they face require finding greater-than-average sources of energy and determination to achieve much of what able-bodied people take for granted. Often, this ultimately translates into a lifetime of superior performance in whatever endeavor people with disabilities choose to pursue.

If you have watched my Labor Day Telethon over the years, you know exactly what I am talking about. Annually, we introduce to tens of millions of Americans people whose accomplishments would distinguish them regardless of their physical conditions—top-ranking executives, physicians, scientists, lawyers, musicians, and artists. The message I hope the audience receives is not that these extraordinary individuals have achieved what they have by overcoming a dreadful disadvantage that the rest of us are lucky not to have to endure. Rather, I hope our viewers reflect on the fact that these outstanding people have been ennobled and strengthened by the tremendous challenges they have faced.

In 1992, MDA, which has grown over the past four decades into one of the world's leading voluntary health agencies, established a personal achievement awards program to demonstrate to the nation that the distinctive qualities of people with disabilities are by no means confined to the famous. What could have been more appropriate or timely in that year of the implementation of the 1990 Americans with Disabilities Act than to take an action that could perhaps finally achieve the alteration of public perception of disability, which MDA had struggled over four decades to achieve?

On Labor Day, 1992, it was my privilege to introduce to America MDA's inaugural national personal achievement award winner, Steve Mikita, assistant attorney general of the state of Utah. Steve graduated magna cum laude from Duke University as its first wheelchair student in history and was subsequently named the outstanding young lawyer of the year by the Utah Bar Association. After he spoke on the Telethon with an eloquence that caused phones to light up from coast to coast, people asked me where he had been all this time and why they had not known of him before, so deeply impressed were they by him. I answered that he and thousands like him have been here all along. We just have not adequately *noticed* them.

It is my fervent hope that we can eliminate indifference once and for all and make it possible for all of our fellow citizens with disabilities to gain their rightfully high place in our society.

ON FACING CHALLENGES

John Callahan

I was paralyzed for life in 1972, at the age of 21. A friend and I were driving in a Volkswagen on a hot July night, when he smashed the car at full speed into a utility pole. He suffered only minor injuries. But my spinal cord was severed during the crash, leaving me without any feeling from my diaphragm downward. The only muscles I could move were some in my upper body and arms, and I could also extend my fingers. After spending a lot of time in physical therapy, it became possible for me to grasp a pen.

I've always loved to draw. When I was a kid, I made pictures of everything from Daffy Duck (one of my lifelong role models) to caricatures of my teachers and friends. I've always been a people watcher, it seems; and I've always looked at the world in a sort of skewed way. Everything I see just happens to translate immediately into humor. And so, humor has become my way of coping. As the years have gone by, I have developed a tremendous drive to express my humor by drawing cartoons.

The key to cartooning is to put a different spin on the expected, the normal. And that's one reason why many of my cartoons deal with the disabled: amputees, quadriplegics, paraplegics, the blind. The public is not used to seeing them in cartoons.

But there's another reason why my subjects are often disabled men and women. I'm sick and tired of people who presume to speak for the disabled. Call me a cripple, call me a gimp, call me paralyzed for life.

Just don't call me something I'm not. I'm not "differently abled," and my cartoons show that disabled people should not be treated any differently than anyone else.

All of the men, women, and children who are profiled in the Great Achievers series share this in common: their various handicaps have not prevented them from accomplishing great things. Their life stories are worth knowing about because they have found the strength and courage to develop their talents and to follow their dreams as fully as they can.

Whether able-bodied or disabled, a person must strive to overcome obstacles. There's nothing greater than to see a person who faces challenges and conquers them, regardless of his or her limitations.

On November 9, 1987, Bob Dole, dwarfed by an American flag, addresses the people of Russell, Kansas, reassuring them that he will not shirk from making unpopular choices if he is elected president.

1

"To Go the Distance"

ON NOVEMBER 9, 1987, despite the chilling 30-degree wind, the cheering crowd anxiously waited for the guest speaker to arrive. Five thousand strong, the multitude almost equaled the entire population of Russell, Kansas. As the Russell High School Bronco Marching Band launched into the opening bars of "Yankee Doodle Dandy," Senator Bob Dole, Russell's most celebrated native son, strode out of Dawson's Drug Store and ascended the speaker's platform.

In a few minutes, Dole would announce his entry into the race for the 1988 Republican presidential nomination. But first, Russ Townsley, editor of the *Russell Daily News,* stepped to the microphone and began to read the telegram of May 1945 that Dole's parents, Doran and Bina, had received about their son Robert, who had been seriously wounded in combat during World War II.

An exploding shell had torn into the right shoulder of Second Lieutenant Dole while he was engaged in a military offensive just south of Bologna, Italy, to push the German army north, beyond the mountains of Tuscany. The shell had shattered his shoulder and had driven fragments of metal into his upper body. He had been left for dead. Talking about his war injuries many years later, Senator Dole said the shell "crushed my collarbone, punctured a lung and damaged vertebrae, leaving me paralyzed from the neck down."

Even today, Dole has extremely limited use of his right arm. He carries a pen or a rolled-up memo clenched in his right hand most of the time, both to make the hand appear useful and to signal to people that they should refrain from greeting him with a typical right-handed handshake.

The November prairie wind set the thousands of blue and gold balloons dancing around an immense banner reading DOLE: PRESIDENT, as the crowd, memories rekindled by the telegram, focused intently on Senator Dole.

Then Bub Dawson, whose father, Chet, had placed a cigar box marked Bob Dole Fund on his drugstore counter in 1947, began to speak about that special collection for Dole. The people of Russell had poured change and bills amounting to $1,800 (a hefty sum back then) into the cigar box to help finance Dole's surgery. Bob Dole never forgot his hometown's support. He had kept that cigar box nearby as a constant reminder; it had rested in a drawer in his desk in Washington, D.C., for decades.

Today, the townspeople had come through again with their support. This time, however, the cigar box held $135,000, all of which was designated for Dole's campaign for the Republican presidential nomination.

With such grassroots support, everyone, including Dole, seemed exhilarated. The other Republican senator from Kansas, Nancy Landon Kassebaum, the daughter of legendary Kansas governor Alf Landon, began to introduce Dole when the crowd exploded into a chant of "Dole! Dole! Dole!" Then the band struck up a victory song. Behind the platform, Doran Dole's old grain elevator glistened in the sun. Senator Dole started his announcement speech.

In November 1987, Bob Dole and his wife, Elizabeth Hanford Dole, greet the people of Bob's hometown, Russell, Kansas, during his second campaign for the Republican presidential nomination. Dole had campaigned for the nomination once before, in 1980, but he lost to former governor Ronald Reagan of California.

"I offer a willingness to work hard, to hang tough, to go the distance," Dole pledged.

No one who knew Dole could doubt his words. Identifying with "America's great heartland presidents," such as Abraham Lincoln, Harry Truman, and Ronald Reagan, Dole spoke of the hard choices they had had to make. He, too, vowed not to shirk from unpopular choices.

As president, Dole said, he would "sit down with congressional leaders . . . and we will stay there as long as it takes . . . until we come up with . . . a new compact that ends with a balanced budget in the near future. . . ."

On the following day, the country's newspaper headlines put Dole's speech in the spotlight. The *Washington Post,* for example, announced, DOLE STRESSES AUSTERITY AS THEME FOR '88. Those who had listened to the speech in Russell, however, were more likely to remember the cigar box.

Americans already recognized Senator Bob Dole as one of the most powerful Republicans in Washington, D.C. He commanded respect. Although he had moved from majority leader in the Senate in 1984 to minority leader a year later when the GOP (Grand Old Party; that is, Republican) no longer had a majority of members, Dole held fast to his position as senatorial spokesman for his party. Dole was a newsmaker: when he spoke, people listened. His speeches voiced the Republican views on such important issues of the day as homelessness, the disabled, foreign policy, and health care.

Behind the scenes, Dole set about gathering (and pressuring) votes in the Senate, enough, he hoped, to pass whatever bill he happened to be pushing. It was not an easy job.

Since 1984, Dole has reigned as one of the most prominent Republicans in the country. Previously, in 1981, he served as chairman of the influential Senate Finance Committee. Because it controls approximately half of the federal budget—a vast sum of money that is funneled to Medicare, Social Security, and other major entitlement programs—the Senate Finance Committee stands as the most powerful committee in the Senate.

Senator Nancy Landon Kassebaum of Kansas (left) and Dole are besieged by reporters in Washington, D.C., after meeting with President Reagan in 1986. Senator Kassebaum, daughter of former Kansas governor Alf Landon, introduced Dole to the chanting crowd in November 1987 when he made his announcement that he would seek the Republican presidential nomination.

In fact, Dole's willingness to be outspoken has garnered him attention, both positive and negative, since the early days of his political career. When he arrived on Capitol Hill, he burst onto the national political scene as a force to be reckoned with. Elected to the U.S. Congress in 1960, he witnessed government scandals up close. Never one to avoid controversy when he saw some advantage for his party, Dole often made the first public call for an investigation into some alleged wrongdoing. As a freshman member of the U.S. House of Representatives during President John F. Kennedy's time in office, Dole had, as Richard Ben Cramer wrote in his 1992 book *What It Takes: The Way to the White House,* "socked the Kennedy White House with its first taste of scandal" concerning Billy Sol Estes in 1961.

Billy Sol Estes, a Texas friend of Vice President Lyndon Johnson's, was arrested by the Federal Bureau of Investigation (FBI) in 1962 for fraud, largely because Dole called for a congressional investigation into the alleged ties between Estes and Johnson and the Agriculture Department's involvement in Estes's farming and business affairs. Dole suspected the Kennedy administration of being tied too closely to Estes's fraudulent mortgages for grain storing. In a complex network of financial wheeling and dealing, Estes had cheated farmers out of their land by means of fake leases to Kennedy's Department of Agriculture.

Dole maintained that the Kennedy administration, which had denied any links between Estes and Lyndon Johnson, had deceived the public. Estes was later found guilty of mail fraud and of swindling $24 million in mortgage deals.

In 1969, one year after Dole was elected to the U.S. Senate, he became a strong supporter of President Richard M. Nixon. In one of Dole's early moves as a senator, he championed two of Nixon's nominees for a vacancy on the Supreme Court in 1969, Clement Haynesworth and then

G. Harrold Carswell. Both were deemed unacceptable by the labor and civil rights groups that had fought to undermine their appointments. Neither nominee made it past the Senate confirmation hearings because of the heated opposition, but Dole had drawn attention to himself as a strong, vocal partisan. Democratic senator Ernest Hollings of South Carolina told Dole, "You've got guts." Senior Republican senators, such as minority leader Hugh Scott, were appalled by Dole's intense and often cocky revamping of some of the Senate's most hallowed, though unwritten, rules, such as being seen and not heard during one's freshman year.

Disapproval from his colleagues, however, did not deter Dole from defending President Nixon at every opportunity. Dole appreciated Nixon's conservative, anticommunist politics. But more than that, the two national figures shared humble origins. Nixon and Dole had risen from similar middle-class roots: Nixon's father had been a grocer and Dole's had operated a cream-and-egg station, where he acted as the middleman between farmers and local merchants. Both politicians lacked the wealth and Ivy League education that boosted the careers of John F. Kennedy and George Bush, among others. In addition, Dole and Nixon were keenly aware of how far they had come on their own. Tenacious fighters, both had reached the political heights with an edge of bitter resentfulness.

Moreover, Nixon exhibited a rare sensitivity in handling Dole's war injury. He was the first person in Washington to offer Dole a left-handed handshake, no doubt because he understood Dole's pride and vulnerability.

In fact, Dole proved so fierce in his defense of President Nixon—he would publicly denounce anyone who criticized the president—that he was dubbed "Nixon's Doberman pinscher" on the floor of the Senate. (Dobermans are known for their loyalty and for their ferocity; they intimidate people and are often seen in movies and television programs guarding a villain's estate.)

Dole's aggressively protective stance toward President Nixon was sorely tested during the Watergate scandal from 1972 to 1974. With his characteristic dry humor, Dole often remarked, "Musta been my night off," when referring to the night of the June 1972 break-in at the Democratic party national headquarters in the Watergate office complex. Dole waited until the very end of the crisis—which shook the political foundations of the country and led to charges of a cover-up that had been ordered by Nixon himself—to abandon the president, as senators from both parties clamored for Nixon's impeachment.

Perhaps Dole could not forget that in 1868 Senator Edmund Gibson Ross from his own state of Kansas had cast the deciding vote to acquit President Andrew Johnson, who had already been impeached by the House of Representatives for violating the Tenure of Office Act by removing an official (Secretary of War Edwin M. Stanton) without congressional consent. (In the federal government, an accused civil official can be removed from office in a two-part process: constitutional authority to impeach a civil official is vested in the House of Representatives, which then commits the accused's case for trial in the Senate.)

President Nixon's resignation on August 8, 1974, saved Dole from having to take a similar stand. When he spoke at Nixon's funeral in April 1994, Dole imparted a sense of loss and depicted Nixon as the quintessential American. Dole's reminiscences of the former leader brought tears to his eyes. His display of emotion surprised some people, but not those who knew him well.

Indeed, in 1976, kicking off his vice-presidential campaign in Russell, Dole broke into tears during his speech when he remembered everything that the townspeople had done for him. To break the silence, President Gerald Ford tactfully rose to his feet and began to clap, and soon the audience began to cheer. To many of Dole's followers, it seemed that his 1975 marriage to Elizabeth "Liddy"

Hanford, his second wife, had softened his steely political manner. An ambitious and accomplished woman in her own right, Elizabeth rivals her husband in hours worked per day. She was a commissioner of the Federal Trade Commission under Nixon, secretary of transportation under Reagan, secretary of labor under Bush, and in 1990, she became the head of the American Red Cross. During the 1984 GOP convention in Dallas, Texas, campaign buttons reading "Dole & Dole in '88" surfaced. The slogan was not entirely a joke; many observers believed that someday the Doles might run together on a ticket.

The low-keyed tone of Dole's campaign for the Republican nomination for president in 1980, however, fell flat. He became too absorbed in Senate matters to totally commit himself to what he called the five Ms—money, manpower, management, media, and momentum—of his campaign. After finishing last in two crucial hurdles, the Iowa and New Hampshire primaries, he dropped out of the race in March 1980.

Ronald Reagan, to whom Dole had compared himself during the campaign by calling himself "a Ronald Reagan who's ten years younger," won the Republican presidential nomination and ultimately the presidency. Dole turned his attention to his campaign for reelection to the Senate, which he won.

The voters did not respond well to Dole's handling of himself in his unsuccessful 1980 presidential bid; nor did he believe he had marketed himself effectively. Reflecting bitterly on Elizabeth's advice to soften his harsh manner by revealing his vulnerability, Dole complained how "She wanted me to take off my shirt, show 'em my arm, and say, 'Here, this is what I did for my country. Now, vote for me.'" By 1991, however, Dole had come to terms with the degree of openness he would be comfortable using politically. "I don't go around parading myself as a disabled veteran or something, but at the same time I think there are ways you can communicate it."

At certain points in the campaign for the 1988 Republican presidential nomination, Dole was considered by many as the Republican with the most support from Democrats and independents. Together, these groups constituted a majority of voters in the United States. As a result, the polls deemed Dole "the most electable Republican" in the nation. Dole's genuine feeling for the people on the street or on the farm had a lot to do with his popularity. He understood how they felt, and he perceived what they had come to realize: that the Reagan years had left many middle- and lower-class Americans behind. These Americans did not share in the prosperity enjoyed by others in the country, and Dole could relate to this harsh reality. He had known hardship firsthand. Years before, as a young county attorney in Kansas, he had had the task of authorizing monthly welfare checks, one of which went to his own grandfather, a tenant farmer who had lost his land. "My grandmother passed away at age 47," Dole told Ruth Shalit in a March 1995 interview for the *New York Times Magazine.* "My grandfather . . . couldn't find work. Times were tough. You don't forget those things."

Dole had crossed the country in 1986 helping to push forward the GOP's congressional candidates. These state elections would determine which party, Democratic or Republican, would have a majority in the House of Representatives and the Senate. Of course Dole had a vested interest in maintaining the GOP majority in the Senate: He would remain majority leader only if enough Republican candidates won. Dole traveled through 21 states in two weeks. As election day neared and the pressure mounted, he urged his staff to put out a press release about all he was doing for the GOP. As it happened, the newspapers decided to print a story about Vice President George Bush, later Dole's Republican rival for the 1988 presidential nomination, and the assistance he had given in the campaign, including details of the number of miles Bush had flown and the amount of campaign money he had raised.

In fact, Dole had done much more than Bush, but his campaign managers had lagged behind Bush's in presenting the complete story to the newspapers. To be a master in the art of politics, in addition to having a sincere understanding of people, one should know how to manage publicity. Organization is the foundation of political expertise, while political canniness and tact (knowing what to say, how to say it, and when to say it) play less concrete roles but are just as important. Organization and timing are imperative for a candidate to make the news; hard work is usually not enough.

Once the campaign for the 1988 Republican presidential nomination was in full swing, Dole and Bush emerged as the two major contenders. After Dole had pounded Bush (who had led in the polls before the Iowa caucus) by a two-to-one margin in the crucial Iowa caucus vote, the campaign got rougher. The New Hampshire primary came next. Bush, an easterner and a graduate of Phillips Academy (in Andover, Massachusetts) and Yale University (in New Haven, Connecticut), fought back after the Iowa primary by running a negative television ad that portrayed Dole as a two-faced fence straddler who did not keep his word—especially concerning taxes. Bush could get away with such an ad because he was considered to be a "nice guy," unlike Dole, who had a reputation for being mean-spirited. (Dole's sharp one-line retorts, honed in Russell, were not as well received in the world of politics. His words sometimes seemed rough, and not many forgot his harsh defense of President Nixon.)

Dole had begun to catch up to Bush in the polls even before he won in Iowa. He climbed 18 points in three days after the Iowa caucus. He was still surging when Alexander Haig, another Republican candidate, bowed out of the race and decided to back Dole. A video clip of Haig's endorsement played over and over again on television.

During the New Hampshire primary, Bush ran the "Senator Straddle" ad. Not only did it focus on Dole's straddling on the issue of taxes but it also combined powerfully with visual images of Bush throwing snowballs and driving a forklift, activities Dole could not do easily because of his war injury.

Soon after the ad was aired, Dole was subjected to a painful public moment. During a live televised debate in New Hampshire, whose residents are traditionally opposed to tax increases, Pete du Pont, another Republican candidate, violated debate rules by presenting Dole with a no-new-tax pledge and challenged him to sign it on the spot. Dole demurred. He literally could not hold the paper down and sign, nor could he read it without his glasses. He offered a joke instead: "Give it to George [Bush] . . . I'll have to read it first." (Dole was referring to the 1987 Intermediate-Range Nuclear Forces treaty that he refused to sign before reading, whereas Bush had supported the

Dole campaigns in New Hampshire prior to that state's Republican presidential primary in February 1988. It was during the New Hampshire primary that Dole's major rival for the nomination, Vice President George Bush, ran the "Senator Straddle" ad, which stressed Dole's straddling on taxes.

agreement before even seeing it.) Dole looked bad in the public's eye; it seemed that Bush's ad attacking Dole as a big taxer might ring true.

Dole lost the New Hampshire primary. His advisers rallied around him and urged him to continue (even though he needed to raise thousands of dollars more in campaign funds), but Dole realized he had lost more than the primary. He had also lost momentum.

That same evening of the New Hampshire primary, NBC news anchor Tom Brokaw interviewed Bush and Dole on television. Dole was hooked up live from his hotel room by satellite, while Bush sat next to Brokaw in the television studio. Dole did not know that Bush was with Brokaw; he could only see the television camera, not the picture that was being broadcast. When asked by Brokaw if he had any message for Dole, Bush replied, "Naw, just wish him well." Dole had not heard Bush's response. Nor was he aware when he was asked the same question that Bush could hear his reply: "Yeah. Stop lying about my record."

Losing the 1988 Republican nomination to Bush devastated Dole. He later recalled, "We sat on our hands for three days trying to decide what to do [about Bush's campaign commercials depicting Dole as a big taxer]. We ended up doing nothing." He also said he blamed the snow for his defeat in New Hampshire: "George Bush was out doing all these physical things, shoveling snow . . . I was walking around a supermarket. . . . My own view of '88 was that I wasn't involved enough. I probably should have micro-managed."

Bush had run successfully for president while continually saying, "Read my lips. No new taxes." Ironically, it was President Bush who broke his no-new-tax pledge in 1990 by raising taxes. Bush even asked Dole to play a significant role in shaping the legislation authorizing the tax increase, and Dole agreed to assist in hammering out the details in Congress.

Dole and Travis York of New Hampshire hold up a T-shirt the eight-year-old had worn while playing the part of Senator Dole in a school play. Travis presented the shirt to Dole, who lost the Republican New Hampshire primary to Bush.

Paul Jacobson, who served as Dole's New England spokesperson during the 1988 campaign, said of this tax increase two years later, "the tax turnaround is bitterly ironic. Dole can't say it, but I can say it: Bob Dole had the courage to lay out the situation of the federal deficit in New Hampshire, while the Bush campaign took the more politically expedient route." Moreover, Michael Kramer reported in *Time* magazine in April 1995, that Bush had determined to do and say "whatever it takes" to win. After having won the presidency in 1988, Bush explained, "The people are wonderful at understanding when a campaign ends and the world of business begins."

More than anything, Dole wanted to remain a player in politics after his loss in 1988. If it required him to swallow his pride and to reach down inside himself for still more determination and energy, it would not be the first time he had done so in his life. It probably would not be the last time, either. Dole is ambitious and tenacious above all—a seasoned warrior who refuses to beat a retreat.

In the late 1920s, Bob (left) and his brother, Kenny, pose before the family car. Bob grew up in Russell, Kansas, in farm country, where his father ran a cream-and-egg station. The Dole boys often helped their father, Doran, load cans of sour cream onto the railroad cars of the Union Pacific for shipment east.

2

THE HEARTLAND

WHEN BOB DOLE SAYS, "Places shape people, Kansas more distinctively than most," he speaks for all Kansans, not just for himself.

Dole was born in the heartland of the United States, on the flat, wind-swept prairie of Russell, Kansas. Through the years, the prairie, which challenges anyone who seeks to eke out a living from its soil, has been overrun by tornadoes, dust storms, swarms of grasshoppers, and mammoth snowstorms. The early settlers of Kansas found that no trees would grow in the earth, so they dug fenceposts out of the region's honey-colored limestone to mark boundaries. Most of these stone markers, called post rocks, still survive today.

Russell's original name, Fossil Station, celebrated the town's founding on the amber-colored rocks. Fossil Station became a stopping place for pioneers ploughing west along the Butterfield Overland Dispatch Trail, formerly the Smoky Hill Trail, which had been created by the Delaware Indians. Herds of buffalo and antelope roamed freely in the area.

The Union Pacific Railroad arrived at Fossil Station in 1867, furnishing a link between the Missouri River and Denver, Colorado. After the Civil War, settlers like Elva and Joseph Talbott and Margaret and Robert Dole—Senator Dole's grandparents—tried to till the soil, build a schoolhouse, and civilize the region. In 1871, soon after the Civil War, the new residents met and voted to rename the town Russell in honor of Captain Avra Russell, a Union war hero from Kansas.

The people of Russell still pride themselves on their endurance. In fact, the Kansas state motto, *Ad astra, per aspera* (To the stars, through difficulties), echoes the strong-willed philosophy of its inhabitants. Bob Dole's parents and grandparents labored long, hard hours each day. Dole's father, Doran, missed only one day of work in his 40-year career of dawn-to-dusk labor. His day at the cream-and-egg station began at 6:00 A.M. and often ended at sundown. On Saturday, he often worked past midnight because that was the day farmers came into town with their produce. In later years, when Doran managed the Norris Grain Company's grain elevator, his workday could run as late as 2:00 A.M. when the harvest came in.

Doran and Bina Dole had four children in quick succession: the oldest, Gloria, was born in 1921; next came Robert, on July 22, 1923; Kenny was born 14 months later, in 1924; and finally, Norma Jean arrived in 1925.

When they were young, Doran's children would race through their school lunches so they could cover for him at work, enabling him to take a short break to eat his own lunch. The pace of life was steady and unrelenting; everyone in the family had to do their share of the work.

Bina kept a scrupulously clean house. She even waxed the floor of the front porch of the Doles' simple three-room home. Like her husband, Bina worked extremely hard. At a time when most mothers stayed at home with their children, Bina set out every day to sell Singer sewing machines door-to-door or from farm to farm. Never one

Bob was born on July 22, 1923, in this house, which had three rooms—a living room, a bedroom, and a lean-to kitchen. The small house, located near the tracks of the Union Pacific Railroad in Russell's less stylish North Side, was home to Bina and Doran Dole and their four children.

to give up easily, she would offer sewing lessons to whomever did not know how to sew, or she would demonstrate to skeptics right then and there how helpful the machine could be. Not surprisingly, she sold a lot of machines.

Bina's persistent determination extended quite naturally to her family: she served a complete dinner followed by a homemade dessert baked by Gloria or Norma Jean and used a tablecloth every night. Bina initiated the idea of handmade Christmas decorations and outside Christmas lights in Russell for the dark December nights. Sometimes she would stay up until 4:00 A.M. sewing a dress for one of her daughters. There seemed to be no limit to her energy.

Bina's second child, Robert Joseph, who was named after his grandfathers, was born in 1923, the same year that oil was discovered in Russell on the Carrie Oswald No. 1 site. The discovery of oil provided a boom for some local residents, as well as outsiders, but it did not do much for the Doles. All four of the Dole children shared one bedroom in the modest house, which stood near the tracks of the Union Pacific Railroad. They shared more than a room—there was just one bike and only a single pair of roller skates. An early aspiration of Bob Dole's was to be able to buy a new bike for the family someday.

Soon after Bob turned nine, the family moved down the street to a larger, more impressive house (one that Dole still owns) at 1035 North Maple Street. But this change of address did not end the Doles' hardships. Kenny, who shared a bed with Bob at the time, had contracted an infection in his leg. These were the days before antibiotics were discovered, so the doctors' attempts to treat Kenny's infection sound very old-fashioned by today's standards: First they soaked bread in hot milk and placed it on the wound to draw out the infection; then Kenny's leg was lanced to drain the fluids, but the laceration broke open again. As a last resort, maggots were sown inside his leg to eat away the infection. When this, too, failed to heal the wound, Kenny was admitted to a hospital located about 30 miles away. The doctors there said the leg would mend, but slowly. Kenny had to use crutches for almost four years. The Doles paid for the doctors' medical fees by bartering goods such as chickens or eggs.

While sleeping next to Kenny and listening to the sounds of the maggots, as well as to his parents' conversations as they tried to figure out how they could pay the doctors, Bob learned about the hardship that sickness

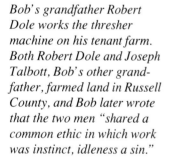

Bob's grandfather Robert Dole works the thresher machine on his tenant farm. Both Robert Dole and Joseph Talbott, Bob's other grandfather, farmed land in Russell County, and Bob later wrote that the two men "shared a common ethic in which work was instinct, idleness a sin."

causes. Young Bob resolved to be persistent, to be a survivor.

Beginning in the early years of the Great Depression, when the American economy collapsed and millions of people lost their jobs, Russell suffered a drought, and dust storms swept through the town for weeks on end. The big prairie sky became black from the dust blocking out the sun, and dust clouds covered everything and everyone. The winds of the Great Plains blew away the soil, transforming parts of Kansas, Colorado, New Mexico, Oklahoma, and Texas into the so-called Dust Bowl. Some residents of these areas believed that the dust storms represented the end of the world, a judgment upon them by the Almighty. When the winds started, 10-year-old Bob and his brother would sprint home from school to beat the storm and then wedge wet towels around all the windows and doors. Despite these precautions, everything inside the house would have to be washed the next day. Bina's spotless home, which, Dole later joked, was so clean that a person could eat off the floors, was invaded by dust. Neighbors, he said, "scooped dirt out of houses with wheat shovels."

When he was 12, Bob began working at Dawson's Drugstore as a soda jerk. By then he was already an experienced worker: he had milked cows at dawn, washed cars, dug dandelions, and sold Cloverine Salve, all for pay. One job that he and Kenny had was delivering handbills on weekends to the 800 houses in Russell. Unlike a paper route, which allows for a quick toss of the newspaper onto the lawn, these handbills had to be given directly to the residents or carefully placed behind their screen doors.

When Bob began working at Dawson's Drugstore, he noticed that the town's doctors who came into the store merited deep respect. In particular, the Doles' family doctor, Dr. Koerber, became an early role model of Bob's. Bob saw how much these physicians gave of themselves

Bob, wearing overalls, is photographed in his teens at 1035 North Maple Street, the home the Doles bought in the early 1930s. After Bob started working at the popular Dawson's Drugstore as a soda jerk, he was able to match the witty style of the Dawson brothers, who were known for their sharp one-liners.

to the community, and he decided that he, too, would become a doctor someday.

Meanwhile, Bob joined in the rough humor at the drugstore, zinging one-liners to the delight of Dawson's customers. If someone asked Bob a question, Chet or Bub Dawson would chime in from some corner of the store, "Why you askin' Bob? He's just the soda jerk." Bob's reply came without missing a beat: "Well, somebody had to have the intelligence to mix a milkshake 'round here."

Dawson's Drugstore functioned as the hub of the town. People would come in to fill a prescription, pick up some toothpaste or a newspaper, or sit down for a cup of coffee. All the townspeople at one time or another found themselves at Dawson's. Many came in to catch up on the news of the day. After Bob started to work there, everybody became acquainted with him.

One day in 1937, when her children came home from school, Bina told them to gather all their belongings and take them down to the basement. An oil prospector had rented the upstairs of the house for one year, and he paid cash in advance. It was an offer Bina found impossible to resist. Of course, the children cooperated immediately because the renters had to move in right away.

Difficulties such as these only toughened Bob Dole. He had two choices: he could sink or swim. He chose to be a success, and he rose to the occasion. His gritty determination even carried over to the area of sports. He awakened early and jogged around town at 5:30 A.M., long before jogging became a popular activity. He was up and about well before most of the other people in Russell.

Bob tried to improve his athletic talent by training rigorously. "Whatever I lacked in natural athletic gifts, I tried to compensate for with willpower," he said in *The Doles: Unlimited Partners,* a book cowritten with his wife, Elizabeth, and published in 1988. This willpower would save him in the trials to come.

Bob and his brother, Kenny, constructed a homemade but very effective set of barbells. They shaped the weighted ends by pouring concrete into cans, then stuck a metal bar between the two concrete blocks.

Bob circled the school track for one mile after his two-hour football practice to prepare himself even further. He also ran on the track team, specializing in the 440- and 880-meter distances.

Frequently alongside him sped Russell's star of the track team, Warren Cooksey. Bob, always one to take a lesson to heart, noticed that Warren, an African American, endured what Dole later recalled as "second-class treatment in some towns on the track circuit." Angered by the prejudice, Bob asked himself, "If a man could be accepted on the running track for his talent alone, how could he be denied equal treatment in the race of life?" This early view of racial prejudice influenced Dole's perspective on the civil rights legislation that he would vote on as a member of the U.S. Congress.

Bob also picked up some political skills from watching his father interact with the farmers and merchants while at work. Although Dole later said in an interview, "I'm certain my parents never gave politics five minutes' thought a month," his father, Doran, would listen carefully to the problems and the new ideas of others. He had an ease about him, even while he maintained his authority. About his father, Dole declared, "He cracked jokes and kept his dignity." Doran also kept himself ready to make a deal. He never forgot a name either, a quality he passed on to Bob, who became widely admired in political circles for this skill. In *Unlimited Partners,* Dole described his father's philosophy:

My father divided the world into two camps. As he put it, "There are doers and there are stewers." If you were on a sinking ship, some people would sit around stewing about the impending disaster, others would get up and do something about it. He didn't have to add that if the doer

Bob Dole (left) and a teammate pose with their high school basketball coach. Bob enjoyed sports, especially track and football, and later said, "Whatever I lacked in natural athletic gifts, I tried to compensate for with willpower."

succeeded in radioing for help, he needn't expect a ticker-tape parade when he returned to port. Why make a fuss over doing your duty?

Dole's mother, Bina, endowed him with a penchant for formal, rather elegant dress. Even today, Dole tends to dress in an impeccable dark suit, a crisp white shirt, and a tie. Although some people might find his mode of dress to be intimidating, Dole acquired the practice from his mother, who wanted everything to be proper.

Bob Dole took his studies seriously and performed well at Russell High School. He preferred history to math and Latin. "Latin verbs seemed pretty pale stuff beside the shoot-'em-up heroics of Bleeding Kansas and the farm revolt of Populist days," he later recalled. Bob worked as sports editor for the student newspaper, *The Pony Express,* and was elected a member of the National Honor Society. He was not so studious, however, that he was beyond trying to get out of taking a test. Bob once brought a five-gallon container of ice cream to his high school journalism class on a test day. The teacher took the bait, and everyone ate ice cream instead of sweating through the exam.

In *Unlimited Partners,* Dole declared that "farmers live out a paradox." He described how very hard they must work in spite of being continually at the mercy of the weather and governmental actions. The foreign strain of Turkey Red wheat brought to Kansas by Volga Germans from the Ukraine was able to withstand severe winters, searing hot summers, and terrible droughts to produce the "amber waves of grain" that were immortalized in Katharine Lee Bates's poem "America the Beautiful." The resilience of the wheat growing in Russell, Kansas, the very center of the United States, symbolizes the stubborn triumph of spirit that Americans like to believe is a quintessentially American trait.

Such spirit could be observed in young Dole, especially when he tried out for the football team. He played end and

In 1941, Dole breaks the tape in a track meet as a freshman at the University of Kansas in Lawrence. He became the first member of his family to attend college, and he entered the pre-med program.

earned a varsity letter. In one notable game, he "threw and caught his own pass and scored a touchdown."

Dole was ready to move on after graduating from Russell High in June 1941. He set his sights on being the first in his family to attend college. He had obtained a $300 bank loan to enroll in the pre-med program at the University of Kansas in Lawrence, which was 200 miles from the house where the Doles lived. He was also attracted to the university basketball team, coached by the renowned Forrest "Phog" Allen, one of the founders of modern basketball.

World War II had begun in Europe in September 1939, and the Nazis were spreading terror throughout Europe and condemning millions of Jews to concentration camps. Meanwhile, in Lawrence, Kansas, university students danced their way through the months in quiet trepidation before the United States actually declared war. Dole played a lot of basketball under Coach Allen, and he had a Saturday milk route for which he had to be out delivering milk at 5:00 A.M. In addition, Dole waited on tables at the house of the Kappa Sigma fraternity to which he belonged, earning some pay and all the food he could eat. But on December 7, 1941, the Japanese bombed the U.S. naval base at Pearl Harbor, Hawaii, the United States entered World War II, and Dole's life and the lives of countless others changed forever. Dole began paying less attention to his courses; his grades slipped to mostly Cs, a far cry from his performance in high school. Dole found it difficult to concentrate on his studies with the war being fought. He tried to keep his vision fixed on becoming a doctor for as long as possible. But in December 1942, 19-year-old Dole signed up for the army's Enlisted Reserve Corps. Soon he was headed for basic training in Abilene, Texas.

Dole enlisted in the U.S. Army in December 1942 and entered basic training at Camp Barkley in Abilene, Texas. He also took engineering classes at Brooklyn College in New York, where he became fascinated by the multicultural environment of Flatbush Avenue.

3

A FEVER DREAM
OF PAIN

IN 1942, THE SECOND WORLD WAR continued to rage in Europe, North Africa, and the Pacific. Although Dole did not know exactly what lay ahead for him, he realized that joining the army would be a major turning point in his life. In June 1943, he arrived at Camp Barkley in Abilene and found himself farther from home than he had ever been before. Basic training was rigorous. Daylong marches and combat practice, classes on how to use machine guns, and field instruction kept Dole constantly busy. He achieved peak physical condition. His six-foot-two-inch frame carried 194 pounds when he eventually completed his officer training as a second lieutenant.

Following his stay at Camp Barkley, Dole became a trainee in the Army Medical Corps for six months and then was reassigned to New York's Brooklyn College for engineering classes. Flatbush Avenue, a major thoroughfare in Brooklyn, fascinated Dole. The variety of life, the Jewish and African-American cultures, and all the different accents he heard for the first time introduced him to what he later called "the world in miniature." Then a series of new assignments at Camp Polk in Louisiana, Camp Breckenridge in Kentucky, and Fort Benning in Georgia continued to expand his horizons far beyond those he had known in Kansas.

By December 1944, much of the fighting in Europe had already taken place. Under Chancellor Adolf Hitler, Germany had invaded Poland on September 1, 1939, and then had gone on to occupy Denmark, Norway, the Netherlands, Belgium, Luxembourg, and part of France. The British, whose prime minister was the eloquent Winston Churchill, fought Hitler and his blitzkrieg (lightning war; swift, mechanized, mobile warfare with coordinated forces of the armored division, bombers, and infantry), but they had run dangerously low on supplies and morale. Under President Franklin Delano Roosevelt, the United States began to assist the British with supplies and matériel, becoming, as Roosevelt explained in one of his radio fireside chats with the American people, "the great arsenal of democracy." On June 22, 1941, Hitler invaded the Soviet Union. The following month, Britain and the Soviet Union signed a treaty that assured British aid to the Soviets. On December 5, the German drive on Moscow collapsed. Two days later, the Japanese air force bombed Pearl Harbor. The naval catastrophe at Pearl Harbor devastated much of the U.S. Pacific fleet and took the lives of more than 2,400 Americans.

But the tide was turning against the Axis powers, which included Germany, Italy, and Japan. On June 6, 1944, D day, Allied forces landed on the beaches at Normandy, France, helping to steer the war in favor of the Allies (primarily Great Britain, the Soviet Union, and the United States). On August 25, the Allies liberated Paris, the French capital, from the Germans and resumed their campaign to recapture the entire Italian mainland. In Italy,

In 1944, Dole completed officer training at Georgia's Fort Benning as a second lieutenant, having learned how to throw a grenade and how to use mortars and machine guns.

the Germans began to fall back to their line of defense, called the Gothic Line, which wound through the Apennine mountain range.

The Italian campaign had started with the Allied invasion of Sicily on July 9, 1943, a year and a half before Dole arrived on Italian shores. Italy had surrendered to the Allies on September 8, 1943, the day before American troops were scheduled to land just south of Naples. The Italians' surrender, however, did not deter the Germans from fighting back—they took control of Rome on September 10, after the new Italian government had made peace with the Allies.

The Allies had worked their way up the so-called boot of Italy, regaining territory in an agonizingly slow advance of about one mile per day. Thousands of American soldiers had already been killed and many more would die. The Germans had been ordered to dig in and fight to the bitter end.

Late in February 1945, Dole was sent to the front lines. Assigned to Company I, Third Battalion, Eighty-fifth Mountain Regiment, he served as platoon leader. He commanded 50 men, who made up three rifle squads and a machine gun unit. The Eighty-fifth Mountain Regiment was part of the renowned Tenth Mountain Division. The Tenth Mountain Division's reputation was legendary. Originally, the men of the division were recruited by the National Ski Association. To join the Tenth Mountain Division, each recruit had to have three letters of recommendation; most of the men were graduates of Ivy League colleges and were superb athletes. Two of them—Deveraux Jennings and Ollie Manninen—would later represent the United States on its ski team in the 1948 Olympics. But by 1944, the requirements for the division had changed. Dole's new company had suffered a terrible toll: 183 of its original 200 men became casualties in the campaign up from Naples to the assault on Monte Belvedere in the Apennines north of Florence. The divi-

This 1944 photograph of Dole, who was six feet two inches tall and weighed 194 pounds, was taken shortly before he was sent to Italy to battle the Germans and their fortifications (known as the Gothic Line) spread throughout the Apennine Mountains.

A 155-mm gun blasts on the beach near Anzio, Italy, on March 2, 1944, during the Allies' attack against German troops. The Allies were able to break out of the Anzio beachhead on May 23, finally reaching Rome on June 4, two days before D day, the day the Allies landed in Normandy, France.

sion's strict requirements for recruitment no longer had top priority.

The engagement on Monte Belvedere had been the Tenth Mountain Division's first major assault. It alone had cost the battalion more than 200 dead and 900 casualties. When Dole first arrived at his assignment, Technical Sergeant Frank Carafa headed the Second Platoon, having taken over command on Monte Belvedere after the commander was killed in combat. Dole replaced the platoon leader, but, as he later recounted in *Unlimited Partners,* he felt out of place, as if he were "dropping in on everyone else's party." However, Dole's dignity and his respect for the men eventually won them over. Stanley Kuschik, platoon sergeant and Dole's second in command, recalled in an interview in 1982 that a lot of the officers "weren't worth much. Dole was the best combat leader the platoon had. If he had to take a farmhouse, he went right for it. Never told somebody else to do it. He stayed in front."

From Monte Belvedere, Dole's division was to move northeast toward Bologna through the hills around Monte della Spe and Castel d'Aiano. The goal was to capture Bologna and drive the Germans from the Po Valley. Although Bologna is only 56 miles north of Florence, the Allied armies would take six months to cover that distance. The fighting, which the understated Dole termed "savage," earned him a Purple Heart in March 1945, after a grenade he had thrown exploded near him and wounded him slightly. After that, Dole and his men continued to dig trenches and wait. Sniper and artillery fire punctuated the boredom in the interim.

During this time, Dole used his prairie-honed skill of listening to his men. A young private who had been wounded on Monte Belvedere had returned to the platoon after medical treatment, but his confidence faltered; he believed he had been a coward during some of the fighting and revealed his anxiety to Dole. Dole later said he recognized intuitively that what the private "needed most was a receptive ear. After that morning, he no longer talked of cowardice, real or imagined. Small as it was, the incident taught me that listening can be a form of leadership."

The major spring offensive, called Operation Craftsman (a powerful maneuver designed to push the Germans north of the Po Valley, thereby enabling the Allies to take over northern Italy), had been scheduled to begin April 12, 1945. However, a dense fog moved across the area and prevented Allied planes from taking off to bomb German defenses north of the position of Dole's platoon.

But there was more momentous news on April 12 than the delay of the operation. President Franklin Delano Roosevelt had died after suffering a cerebral hemorrhage at his cottage in Warm Springs, Georgia. The 63-year-old Roosevelt was of special importance for the troops—along with being president, he was also commander in chief of all U.S. military forces. Dole was not the only soldier to mourn his passing.

Operation Craftsman had been rescheduled for April 14 at 6:00 A.M. But the impenetrable fog lingered until 8:00 A.M. By 9:00 A.M. the bombing began. Allied P-47 fighter planes dropped 500-pound bombs on Hill 913, Dole's focal point for the day. He and his men were supposed to take the hill and reach a point three miles to the north. After the heavy bombers were finished, the fighter bombers arrived, along with artillery that fired 75-, 105-, and 155-millimeter shells. Dust and smoke covered the region in what emerged as the most powerful bombing of German positions in the entire Mediterranean theater of war up to that point.

As the smoke began to clear, silence reigned for a few moments. The Germans had previously been informed that the famed Tenth Mountain Division did not take prisoners and that the battle would have to be fought to the death. The Germans had dug themselves an elaborate network of bunkers and gun emplacements on Hill 913. Strategically placed minefields gave them additional protection.

Dole and his men found themselves taking cover behind a hedgerow. An open field called the Pra del Bianco stretched between Dole's platoon position and Hill 913. Machine-gun fire burst from a farmhouse on the left. There was sniper fire, too, "worse than Belvedere," as soldier Al Nencioni later remembered. "Their snipers were good," he declared, "there were a lot of head shots." Dole decided to assemble a small squad to attempt to find a safer route up the hill.

Although Technical Sergeant Frank Carafa should have led the squad into the field according to the original orders, instead Dole launched into the clearing with his squad and his radio operator. Covering fire failed to daunt the Germans, who hit two men. As the radio operator moved to help his comrades, he, too, was hit. Dole, still running on what he later described as "a combination of raw anger and protective instinct for my buddies," crept out to retrieve his radio man, but he was too late. Dole dragged the dead body back to the foxhole.

Dole saw others who needed help, and as soon as he left the shelter of the foxhole his lunge forward was interrupted by an exploding shell, which blasted into his right shoulder and obliterated it. Metal fragments then tore through Dole's body in the shell's wake, causing more injury.

Dole (kneeling, far left, with light-colored coat and no helmet) and his platoon, Company I, Third Battalion, Eighty-fifth Mountain Regiment, pose for this picture in Italy. Dole, as platoon leader, commanded three rifle squads and a machine gun unit.

Dole lay facedown on the ground, surrounded by craters formed by exploding shells. He had no feeling in his arms; at first he thought they had been blown off, when, in fact, they were stretched above his head. He was paralyzed from the neck down; his collarbone had been crushed, and a lung had been punctured. Delirious with pain, Dole began moaning for help. Technical Sergeant Frank Carafa believed that Dole was calling him, so he skittered across the 40 yards separating them and dragged Dole to safety as bullets whizzed around them.

The platoon had to keep moving forward. Orders indicated that the men should leave their wounded behind for the medics, who would soon follow. Two medics who had tried to reach Dole were killed. His platoon realized that few, if any, medics would survive the battle. The Germans shot medics, even though the Geneva Convention, an international agreement signed in 1864 that established a code for wartime care of the sick and wounded, forbade it for humanitarian reasons. Platoon Sergeant Stanley Kuschik, second in command, decided to disobey orders. Dole was "gray, the way they got before they died," Kuschick recalled. "I couldn't just leave him to die by himself."

He administered a dose of morphine that he had taken from a dead medic. He dipped his finger in Dole's blood and painted an "M" on Dole's forehead to alert anyone who might minister to him later that he had already been given a shot of morphine. A second dose could prove fatal.

Sergeant Kuschik further disobeyed orders when he called for Arthur McBryar, a soldier from Dole's platoon, to stay with Dole. McBryar had been slightly wounded in the leg, but he was still considered to be able-bodied. Orders demanded that no healthy soldier remain behind with the wounded. The reason was obvious: able-bodied men were in short supply in the Tenth Mountain Division, which had suffered more casualties that day than all the other Allied forces in Italy combined. The fighting was savage. They needed all their men for battle.

McBryar worried more about Dole's condition than his own. He placed a bandage on Dole's wound to try to stanch the flow of blood. It seeped everywhere—Dole's uniform became dark with blood as did the ground beneath him.

In the meantime, Dole, who had been moaning, finally managed a question through teeth clenched in pain: "How bad is it?" McBryar lifted back the bandage. To his horror, when he looked at what should have been Dole's shoulder he could only see Dole's back. Somehow he offered Dole the reassurance he did not have himself. McBryar cradled Dole's head in his lap, administered a potion of sulfa and water to stave off infection, and talked to him in an effort to keep him conscious—to keep him alive. Dole later recalled this time before the medics arrived as "a fever dream of pain."

The hours passed by. At one point, the German machine gunners had been wounded. McBryar left Dole and tried to find a medic, but he did not succeed. Artillery fire continued around them and McBryar ended up with a concussion during the commotion. Although befuddled by his own wound, McBryar later found medics and led them to Dole. After waiting nine hours, both men were taken to the Fifteenth Evacuation Hospital.

Dole's fever dream of pain began lifting somewhat. He later recounted, "I don't remember much until being in this lineup with a whole lot of litters waiting my turn to go to an Italian hospital where they sort of check to see how you are." When he finally arrived at the hospital, the medical staff did not believe that Dole would survive.

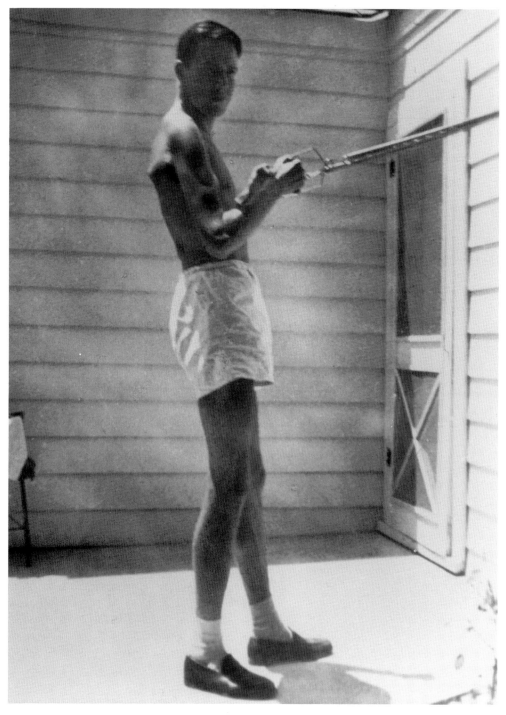

Outside his parents' garage in Russell, Dole uses homemade pulleys and weights to strengthen his arms. When he was injured by an exploding shell on April 14, 1945, Dole could not feed himself or use his hands for nearly one year.

4

THE QUIET BATTLE

THE FIELD HOSPITAL near the battlefield proved to be the first of many hospitals for Dole. While the doctors were making a quick assessment of his injuries, Dole later recalled, he traveled back in his mind to his Russell childhood. He remembered his little white dog, Spitzy, and he pictured his family settled in around the dinner table at home. Dole wrote that the experience was "like watching a movie of my life."

Meanwhile, the doctors recorded the damage from the exploding shell. Dole's injuries rendered him completely paralyzed in his arms and legs. Dole could feel nothing below his neck.

As soon as he was stabilized, he went to a second hospital in Pistoia, a city near Florence. Surgeons in the Pistoia hospital operated on Dole to search for an object that was pressing against his spinal cord. When Captain Woolsey, the presiding physician, examined Dole during the exploratory operation, he found little that he could do for his patient.

The shell had destroyed most of Dole's right shoulder. All that remained for the surgeon to do was to clean out the wound as best he could and sew Dole up. The doctors believed that if Dole survived—and they doubted whether he would—he would never be able to walk again.

Dole's right arm was set in traction and a sling was positioned under his chin to keep his head up. He could only move his dark, intense eyes. Weeks went by. A fellow patient and Kansan from Dole's company visited Dole with another Kansas friend from the company. They talked encouragingly to Dole and helped him relax so he could sleep.

Eventually, Dole healed to the degree that he could be fitted for a body cast, which reached down from his neck all the way to his hips. Although his arms and legs were left free of the cast, he still could not move them. The doctors believed that Dole's best chance for treatment lay in a hospital outside the battle zone, where more special attention could be paid to his injuries. Field hospitals dealt with soldiers immediately after they had been wounded. The care they gave to the injured was lifesaving, but soldiers were then sent on to another hospital for long-term treatment.

The doctors planned to transfer Dole to a hospital ship. However, Dole still had not gone anywhere by May 2, 1945, the date that the German surrender in Italy took effect. The Allies had achieved their goal less than three weeks after Dole had been injured. American troops had crossed the Po River and forced the Germans back behind the Alps. They took over the Brenner Pass, a pivotal crossing point through the high Alps, on their way to meet with other American troops advancing into Germany. On April 27, Benito Mussolini, the Fascist leader of Italy who had declared war on the Allies and had aligned himself with Hitler, was captured in northern Italy by a band of Italian partisans as he and his mistress were fleeing toward Austria. Mussolini was brutally murdered on the following day, April 28. On April 30, Hitler lay dead in his Berlin bunker after committing suicide. The war in Europe was finally over. But for Dole the real battle, the quiet one, lay ahead. Ten days after he was wounded, he had sent a letter (someone had to write it for him) to his parents explaining that he had "a little trouble with my right arm." He even ventured to say he thought he would be as good as new "before long," although there was nothing to base his hopes upon.

A few nights before Dole was scheduled to be shipped to the Seventieth General Hospital in Casablanca, Morocco, in late May, Captain Woolsey called the hospital chief, Colonel Prosser, over to Dole's bed during routine rounds in the hospital ward. Woolsey instructed Dole to show the chief what he could do physically. For a long time nothing happened. Finally, with great effort registering on his face, Dole slowly and deliberately succeeded in raising his left arm four inches. Those four inches constituted an enormous distance for Dole. The doctors were pleased with this improvement.

The Casablanca hospital functioned as a springboard for Dole and others returning to the United States through Miami, Florida. Miami symbolized home, or safety, so the first thing Dole did when he returned to the States was to call his parents. Of course, someone had to hold the phone for him, but he assured his family that he would be back home soon. Only six weeks had passed since he had been injured, but Dole's life had drastically changed.

By June 12, Dole had been sent to the Winter General Army Hospital in Topeka, Kansas, located about 178 miles east of Russell. Bina was waiting for him when he arrived at the hospital. The first sight of her son shocked her to tears. Strong as she usually was, Bina became overwhelmed by the bleak sight of her once-strapping son, who was now seemingly reduced to helplessness. But noting her son's distress at seeing her tears, she vowed never to cry in front of him again. Bina stroked his cheek and then picked eight cigarette butts out of his cast. Someone had used his cast as an ashtray during the trip from Miami. Dole himself had taken up smoking, a habit of which she disapproved, but she bore with it for his sake, even to the extent of lighting his cigarettes and holding them so he could smoke.

Bina moved into an apartment across the street from Winter General. This enabled her to be with her son night and day. She fed him and wiped his chin clean. Dole had lost control of his bowel and bladder functions, and he had a persistent fever that would not break. The doctors held out little hope for any speedy, or full, recovery. It would take a long time before Dole would be able to sit up, let alone walk to the bathroom. But Dole had not yet abandoned his hopes of a full recovery or of playing basketball again under coach Phog Allen back at the University of Kansas. The doctors decreased his body cast by inches when Dole gained some feeling in his left arm and both legs. He could still feel nothing in his right arm, however. Dole's determined efforts caused seizures some days, or a violent shaking spell instead of the progress he craved. The pain of his wound never left him.

In early July, Dole's fever climbed to a dangerous 108.7 degrees Fahrenheit. The doctors were worried that he might die within hours. They told Dole's mother, who summoned his father and his sister Norma Jean. The Russell police force alerted the Topeka police; after flying along Route 40 from Russell to Topeka, the Doles' car sped into the city with a police escort. By the time they arrived, Dole was unable to recognize them.

The doctors tried to combat the fever by packing Dole in ice and wrapping a rubber sheet around him. They also plied him with the new wonder drug called penicillin. As his fever began to drop toward a less dangerous level, the cause of the fever became clear. Unable to urinate, even with a catheter, the doctors discovered that he had a kidney infection. Because Dole, who was unable to move himself,

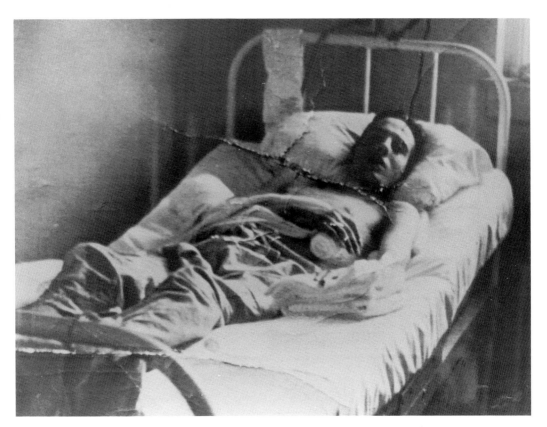

had not been shifted enough by the hospital staff, the sulfa medication he took had come to rest in his kidneys, infecting one of them. The right kidney turned out to contain numerous kidney stones, hard deposits of mineral salts that sometimes form. On July 11, 1945, doctors removed Dole's infected right kidney.

Dole survived this medical crisis. But another, quieter crisis loomed over him. As he began to recover physically, his mind began to catch up with the full import of what had happened to him. Up to this point, the doctors had voiced serious doubts about Dole ever walking again. Nevertheless, Dole had truly believed he would be playing for Coach Allen's team a year from September. Suddenly, his reflections flashed ahead to a vision of himself, "going through life unmarried, selling pencils on street corners

Dole, seen here in one of the many hospitals in which he was treated, had to overcome a number of medical crises, including a dangerous fever and a kidney infection, before he could return home to Russell. By September 1945 he could move his legs, and he slowly began the process of learning how to walk again.

and living off a disability pension," he later wrote. He entertained the bleak prognosis that the medical experts had given him and he tried to envision what this future might be like.

Dole refused to accept that this particular image applied to him. He hung on, despite the feelings of despair and self-pity that he experienced occasionally. Finally, his cast was removed. By September 1945 he could move his legs. The nurses gently placed them over the side of the bed as an early step in his therapy, but even this small movement dizzied him with fatigue. Progress from the bed to a standing position came slowly. Dole shook violently (he had not walked since April), but he persisted and sometimes even flashed a brave smile. Behind the smile, Dole's thoughts and feelings ran deep. As he told *Washingtonian Magazine* in December 1982, "To be completely helpless has a marked effect on anyone. I couldn't feed myself for almost a year, or do anything with my hands."

Soon Dole took a couple of steps—another enormous effort. Watching him take his first hesitant steps, Bina remembered her son learning to walk as a baby of 10 or 11 months. She saw the same determination in him that she had witnessed years before. Nevertheless, this newly acquired freedom held some drawbacks for Dole. At one point, while walking to the bathroom, Dole caught his first glimpse of himself in a mirror since his injury. He was appalled at the sight. He had been completely transformed: His weight had dropped from a healthy 194 pounds to 122. It was an image he would never forget. Even today, Dole tries to avoid looking at himself in a mirror.

Before Thanksgiving Day, Dole traveled hundreds of miles from Russell to the Percy Jones Army Medical Center, a special hospital for orthopedics (the treatment of disorders of the skeletal system), located in Battle Creek, Michigan. The medical center concentrated on treating amputees and paraplegics; it had opened the summer after the Japanese bombed Pearl Harbor. By November 1945, the hospital had grown so large it doubled the population of Russell in size (which in 1941 had 5,003 inhabitants). At the hospital, Dole's right hand was strapped to a special device designed to stretch his fingers back to their former shape. But within weeks of his arrival at Percy Jones, "a deformed hand was the least of my concerns," Dole later recalled. On December 21, he woke up with a horrific pain in his lungs that was caused by a pulmonary infarct, or

Dole (center) is helped out of the house by his father (right) and his grandfather during a leave from the hospital. Dole later said that he was horrified the first time he saw himself in a mirror after his injury—he had lost more than 70 pounds since April 1945.

blood clot, a condition that can prove fatal. This illness was another price Dole had to pay for moving around so little for such a long time.

Doctors prescribed dicumarol to thin his blood. Although it temporarily transformed Dole into a hemophiliac (one whose blood cannot clot and who risks bleeding to death, even from the smallest cut), the potential of uncontrolled bleeding was less dangerous than the clot moving toward his heart. The doctors ordered Dole to be immobile. Doran came from Russell by train to visit his son in Battle Creek on Christmas Day. The train was overflowing with servicemen, so Doran had to stand for several hours; he arrived with badly swollen ankles to see his son, a gesture that still brings tears to Dole's eyes.

Once again, Dole's prognosis seemed grim. When he asked what their prediction was for his improvement, the doctors told him he had a 50-50 chance of survival. He continued to hang on, but all the progress he had made began to wither away as the weeks of inactivity stretched on beyond the new year. The doctors had given him penicillin again to fight another infection, but it was to no avail. The infection moved to his lungs, causing pneumonia. Dole's fever rose to 106 degrees. Throughout his ordeal, Dole's family had driven to Battle Creek several times, a trek that exhausted them. So it was to Dole's visiting brother, Kenny, that the doctors proposed using a new, experimental drug called streptomycin on their patient. Because it was still being tested, hospital protocol required that a consent form be signed by the next of kin; in Dole's case, his parents. They had to come back to the hospital to sign the form.

Dole became one of three U.S. Army patients to receive the so-called wonder drug. Of the other two patients, one had died and the other had gone blind. In Dole's case, the drug helped revive him.

Weeks of hard work followed. His daily routine included whirlpool baths to relax his taut muscles and hot wax treatments on his hands to loosen the fingers that were clenched into claws. Dole literally spent hours struggling to close two fingers of his injured right hand. Once again, he had to learn to walk step by step. Fortunately, his health improved at a steady pace. Just as before, the relative calm in his physical condition allowed Dole to focus on his other struggle, what he called his "quiet battle against the emotional ravages of war."

He witnessed the physical ravages of war every day in the hospital ward. Along with Dole, two other future U.S. senators would emerge from Percy Jones Hospital: Philip A. Hart of Michigan, who had been wounded in the D-day assault on Normandy, and Daniel K. Inouye of Hawaii, who had lost his right arm in combat in Europe. There were still more patients, such as the young air force captain who had been severely hurt in a plane crash and who had remained silent until he uttered a faint gasp one night as he died.

What kept Dole going in part was the awareness that others had suffered from wounds that were even more debilitating than his. Much as Flatbush Avenue in Brooklyn had opened Dole's eyes to multicultural lifestyles, his stay in Percy Jones gave him a deeper understanding of people in general. He learned that appearances can be deceiving and that there are different degrees of helplessness and of courage. When people called him a hero, he replied, "The real heroes didn't come back."

Dole became known in the hospital for his jokes. Russell humor cheered the other patients so much that the nurses wheeled Dole around to other wards. Dole knew the effect his wry humor had on others; it also helped him in his own quiet battle. His recovery was complicated. For example, he took dosages of demerol and morphine to dull the pain, but they weakened the determination that is so vital for success, so he did not want to take the drugs for long. He knew, too, the psychology of pain, saying later, "thinking about how much you hurt makes you hurt more."

Dole moved into his parents' ground-floor bedroom at 1035 North Maple Street when he returned to Russell in late 1946. Initially unable to eat, bathe, or dress himself, Dole had to be satisfied with watching the rest of the family go through their daily routines.

Dole's method of coping was to avoid thinking about the pain. He pushed it down, deep within himself.

Dole waged a continual battle against the feeling of helplessness, which he loathed. As he began to walk again, he would inevitably fall sometimes. When this happened, he always tried to get himself up without help from anyone else. The progress he made enabled him to return to Russell on leave. There he began his own rigorous training. The doctors had done all they could medically; now it was up to him.

Bina brought her son back to the family home in Russell. The doctors had done everything they could for him. Dole understood this, yet he could not accept his limitations. Bina and Doran gave their ground-floor bedroom, located next to the living room, to their son and his hospital bed. From that bedroom, he could look through the French doors to where the family bustled in the living room. Dole enjoyed being back home. Most evenings, his father read aloud to him from the *Salina Journal,* or he listened in on card games his parents and their neighbors played.

But Dole still needed help eating, bathing, dressing, and getting into the bathroom. The neighbors had their own difficulty adjusting to the new, gaunt visage of Dole, who shuffled down the street like an elderly man. They watched as Dole achieved the goals he had set for himself: first a walk up to the corner, then a journey all the way around the block. The Dawson family had told him he could expect a free milkshake the first time he made it all the way to Dawson's Drugstore. He took them up on the challenge.

Doran and Kenny fashioned a system of ropes, pulleys, and weights for Dole to work out with every day. He tried to strengthen his left hand by squeezing a rubber ball. This worked so well that he became strong enough to hold a hand of cards in the evenings when friends came over to visit. A high school buddy, Adolph Reisig, helped Dole undertake a physical therapy regimen. One facet of the therapy involved a 25-pound sleeve of lead, which fit over Dole's right arm. The weight would strengthen his arm while rubber bands held his fingers open. Reisig had made the brace for Dole in his auto body shop.

Dole grew stronger by pushing himself. He even asked Reisig to add more lead to the brace. If it began to hurt, he knew it was working. One day, after Dole's parents had come home from work and had searched everywhere for him, they discovered him trying to straighten his right arm by hanging from the rafters in the garage. While dangling above them, he was soaked with sweat from the effort and the pain. Still, his right arm, which was virtually useless, rested cocked at a sharp right angle.

Although Dole knew how serious his injury was, he persisted in hoping for a miracle. He honestly believed that he would recover and would go back to shooting baskets. In fact, he had consulted with surgeons in three major cities; each one had spoken of impairment and nerve damage, but none offered him the hard news he had to hear. Consequently, when Dole's uncle Lamont Jahn mentioned a Dr. Hampar Kelikian with whom Jahn had served in the Medical Corps, Dole sought Kelikian's advice. Early in 1947, he journeyed to Chicago to meet Kelikian and was taken aback by the doctor, who, he said, "came rushing to greet me in the hallway in broken English. He was hard to understand and I thought, 'Maybe I'm his first patient.'" After World War I, Kelikian had escaped from Armenia with a carpet and the equivalent of $20. In spite of such adversity, he became one of the premier neurosurgeons in the United States. He specialized in the restoration of damaged limbs and was highly respected in the field.

Dr. Kelikian's first task was to realistically determine what could and could not be done for Dole. Yes, he could bring back partial use of Dole's arm; however, Dole would never be able to turn or lift the arm. Dole's shoulder bones had been permanently damaged. His dream of playing basketball crumbled as he listened to Dr. Kelikian. But deep down, Dole was willing to accept what the doctor was telling him. All his hard work, fueled as it had been by gritty determination and hope, had vividly illustrated what his limitations were. Dr. Kelikian's assessment offered the first real measure of hope.

Dr. Kelikian planned the first operation for June 1947. Although Dole did not have to pay the doctor a fee (Kelikian charged only those who could pay their bill), he did have to pay the hospital costs because his medical expenses no longer fell under the army's jurisdiction.

Dr. Kelikian operated three times on Dole during 1947. After the first surgery, on June 3, Dole did not heal properly. Dr. Kelikian's attempt to hang Dole's right arm by a strip of muscle did not free the arm. Instead it hung in the wrong position high on Dole's chest. The second operation, in early August, brought the arm down to Dole's side, where it remains today—a couple of inches shorter than the left arm. The third operation, in November, met with limited success: the doctor's transplant of muscle and tendons to Dole's right hand did not succeed.

Dole would be partially disabled for the rest of his life. He could not rotate or hold anything heavy with his right arm. The fingers of his right hand would remain oddly splayed. He could hold the arm down so it looked quite natural and comfortable, although it required effort to keep it there. He could grasp light objects, such as a pen or a rolled-up sheet of paper, in his right hand. And he would continue to have limited sensation in his left hand (for example, he cannot distinguish a dime from a quarter when he has his eyes shut). The news sobered him, and he later declared, "I don't care who it is, it takes a while to accept you have limitations you didn't have the day before yesterday or the month before."

Dr. Kelikian's assistance offered Dole a new beginning. During an interview on the television program "60 Minutes," which was broadcast on October 24, 1993, Dole recalled that he said to himself, "OK, let's get out of here. Let's start thinking about the future instead of the past, and maybe Bob Dole can do something else."

While he recuperated at Percy Jones Hospital after the third operation, Dole met Phyllis Holden, an occupational therapist, at an officers' club dance at the hospital. She had noticed him before and had been impressed by his intense good looks and his sense of humor. Dole considered Phyllis to be attractive, plus she knew how to treat him. He hated sympathy, and she understood that. They married on June 12, 1948, in her home town of Concord, New Hampshire, three months after their first date. Dole, who earlier had despaired of ever marrying, found a partner who helped him focus on thinking, as he said, "not in terms of disability, but of ability. She treated me like everyone else." Marriage was just what Dole needed to get on with finding that "something else" he could do in life.

Phyllis Holden was an occupational therapist at Percy Jones Army Medical Center in Battle Creek, Michigan, when she met Dole at a dance for the patients in November 1947. He later said, "Phyllis made me forget my injuries. She helped me think, not in terms of disability, but of ability. She treated me like everyone else." They were married in St. Paul's Cathedral in Concord, New Hampshire, in June 1948.

County Attorney Bob Dole and his assistant go through paperwork in Dole's office in the mid-1950s. When he became county attorney in January 1953, Dole handled cases involving bounced checks, speeding tickets, burglaries, and child abuse.

5

A CITIZEN OF KANSAS

DOLE MOVED TO TUCSON, where he enrolled as a junior at the University of Arizona in 1948. The GI Bill, which funded education for veterans, made the Doles' move possible. Dole's doctors had advised him to seek out a warmer, drier climate for his health. He and his wife, Phyllis, drove to Arizona in a car his friend Adolph Reisig had fixed up with a left-handed gearshift.

Dole began his course of study in the liberal arts, although months before he had discussed with Dr. Kelikian the possibility of becoming a lawyer. Dr. Kelikian had been supportive of the idea. A year later, Dole transferred to Washburn University in Topeka, Kansas. There he enrolled in a dual program of undergraduate history and graduate law.

At the beginning of Dole's postwar studies, Phyllis had taken notes for him in his classes. She had also written out the answers to the exams for him while he dictated what she should write. Fortunately, the Veterans Administration bought him one of the first recording machines ever made. The Sound-scriber, as it was called, was the size of a breadbox. Dole set it near the professor and recorded the class lecture; then, back at home, he would write out what he heard in his laboriously slow, left-handed script. The machine had small green disks that he would play over and over until he wrote everything down on paper with his left hand. It usually took him hours to complete. Sometimes it took all night.

Dole was determined to do better than the grades of C and B that he had received as a college student before the war. Given the lessons in determination and discipline he had learned, the only way he could study a subject was to throw himself into it so thoroughly that he mastered it. He paced back and forth in the living room memorizing facts. A fellow student and friend, Sam Crow, came over to study with him. Dole stored his pack of Camel cigarettes rolled up in his T-shirt on his right side, where the shirt sloped radically because of his missing shoulder. Neither student talked about Dole's deformity. Both Dole and Crow had politics on their minds as possible careers, so they took a night course called Beginner's Speech. When Dole held back during class, the speech teacher urged him to try to assert himself more. He followed his teacher's advice and participated more frequently in class. Thus he acquired more confidence in himself.

When Washburn's law librarian, Beth Bowers, suggested he run for the Kansas state legislature in 1950, Dole carefully considered her recommendation. Russell County politicians, Democrats and Republicans alike, encouraged him to pursue political office, too. Dole knew he could transfer the competitive drive he had shown in athletics over to politics; it seemed a "natural substitute," for him, he later said, explaining that "Knocking on a stranger's door, looking him in the eye and asking for his vote was a way to overcome my disability without denying it." He also believed it was one way to repay some of the community support he had received after the war.

The members of Dole's family were registered Democrats; however, John Woelk, Russell County attorney and a Republican, persuaded Dole to run as a Republican. The state of Kansas had more Republicans than Democrats on the rolls, he asserted, and in Russell County, Republicans dominated the number of registered voters by a margin of two to one. Dole decided to switch parties. He beat his rival, the Democratic incumbent Elmo Mahoney, to become, at age 27, Russell County's youngest state legislator to date.

When Dole embarked on his political career, he earned a salary of $5 per day (up to $350 maximum), and $7 per day for expenses during the biennial legislative session. After someone asked about his legislative agenda in Topeka, Dole replied, "I'm going to sit and watch for a couple of days, and then I'll stand up for what I think is right." He took office in January 1951 and joined a legislative session that he later said was "marked by evasion, confusion and occasional bursts of inspiration." One day, for example, the Kansas House of Representatives endorsed voting rights for 18-year-olds; the following day, it reversed the decision.

Dole took his bar exam to practice law in the spring of 1952. As an ambitious young law student, Dole had caught the eye of Russell attorney Eric "Doc" Smith. Smith invited him to join his practice in Russell after Dole passed the bar exam. He told Dole that his war injury did not have to "interfere with a legal career." Dole set up his office as a junior partner over a store at Eighth and Main streets in Russell. A secondhand desk and an impressive leather chair helped to establish him.

Bob and Phyllis moved into a rented house in Russell. Dole worked late every night and all day on Saturdays. Sunday dinners were held at Bina and Doran's house, and Bob and Phyllis always joined the family for these meals. Kenny, Gloria, and Norma Jean lived nearby, so the family frequently saw one another.

The year 1952 became a busy one for Bob Dole. In June, he announced his candidacy for Russell County attorney. His chief supporter, John Woelk, had decided to retire. Dole calculated that if he won the position, he might end up with a secure future as a local attorney. As it turned out, people would later view this race as the real start of Dole's political career and campaign style.

Dole, however, had to win the nomination in the Republican primary first. He ran against Dean Ostrum, the son of a prominent attorney in Russell and a graduate of the prestigious Yale Law School. Ostrum's father was as well known in town as Dole's father was. Dole announced his candidacy in a one-sentence statement that he delivered in a high school gym.

The race evolved into one between rich and poor; while Ostrum downplayed his wealth, Dole simply continued to wear his worn shirts. Having been wounded in combat and being handsome as well, Dole seemed to naturally attract supporters. Unlike the veterans of the Vietnam War in the 1960s and 1970s, who met with a lot of criticism and very little help, veterans from World War II received approval of all kinds, including gratitude and heightened status from the American public. This often translated into an advantage at the polls. Before being elected to the U.S. presidency in 1952, Dwight D. Eisenhower, a fellow Kansan, had been supreme commander of the D-day Allied invasion of Normandy.

In addition, Dole's disability resulted in some highly effective campaigning. His unwillingness to have someone sitting next to him cut up his meat for him at public dinners encouraged Dole to step away from the head tables, where the speakers and officials sat, and to circulate among the other tables. A friendly word spoken here or there benefited him far more than segregating himself with the other officials. He took his discomfort or embarrassment at the head table and transformed it into a smart political move. No one else circulated; they preferred to talk with one another at the speakers' table. Dole was different: he knew the people, many of them by name, and he cared about them.

His phenomenal memory also served him well. He could recall things about people most politicians would never bother about, even if they could remember them. For example, if he heard about a family gathering or a celebration, he would make it a point to appear there briefly and discreetly. He would not try to dominate the occasion but rather participate unobtrusively. The fact that he remembered the occasion delighted people. In turn, they recalled his thoughtfulness on election day.

When campaigning, Dole scoured the county for votes. A light shining in a farmhouse kitchen or parlor was enough to lure him to the door for a chat. He worked from sunup to sundown. Later, when Dean Ostrum was asked how long his day of campaigning had been, he replied, "I

Dole learned a lot about politics from U.S. representative Wint Smith (left) and U.S. senator Frank Carlson (right) and would eventually win both men's seats in Congress (Smith's in 1960 and Carlson's in 1968). This picture was taken in 1956 during a GOP campaign stop in Russell.

don't know, but it wasn't as long as Bob Dole's. I'm sure of that."

Dole needed the job. As he later explained, "I ran against Dean Ostrum, who was a much better lawyer, from a family of lawyers, very fine family. He was probably a lot smarter than I was. But people thought, 'Oh, poor Bob, he needs the job.'" Actually, Dole needed the job for two reasons. First, he required the financial security, but second, he craved the success and the acceptance it implied. By venturing out and talking to every voter he could find, Dole was also showing himself and his arm to people. He could not hide his disability, especially because he could not shake hands with his right hand. In those days, handshakes were as much a part of the social fabric as saying "Have a nice day" is today. If people voted for him, it meant they felt he could do a good, solid job even with his disabled right hand. Dole once said he learned the value of adversity on that fateful morning of April 14, 1945: "A handicap can become an asset, I've since discovered, if it increases your sensitivity to others and gives you the resolve to tap whatever inner resources you have."

Dole's brother, Kenny, and Adolph Reisig tacked up posters all over town and beyond during the campaign for county attorney. Dole himself handed out leaflets on Main Street. He began many speeches by saying he did not grow up with all the advantages, and neither did most of the voters. Meanwhile, his opponent, Ostrum, had grown up with many financial and educational advantages. Dole earned a lot of votes taking this tack while campaigning.

When the big day arrived, Dole received 1,133 votes to Ostrum's 948. It was not a landslide victory, but it was enough to validate Dole politically. He went on to defeat Democrat George Holland by a wider margin in the county election: 4,207 to 2,065 votes. (Ironically, George Holland was the son of Clifford Holland, Sr., an important local Democrat who had previously encouraged Dole to enter politics.)

The county attorney held his position for a two-year term. It paid $248 per month, slightly less than the courthouse janitor's salary. The cases the county attorney handled included the county's civil legal business and criminal prosecutions: speeding tickets, bad checks, DWI (Driving While Intoxicated) arrests, and sporadic burglaries. The most difficult cases for Dole involved taking abused children from their parents and finding new homes for them and signing the welfare checks for county recipients. Dole maintained a small private practice in what little free time he could muster. Handling wills and licenses kept him busy. Most nights he worked late. Often he attended some social gathering and then returned to his office to resume work. The light in his second-floor office of the courthouse burned bright and long. Bub Dawson, who closed his drugstore across the street every evening at 11 P.M., frequently looked up and saw Dole's light on at that hour. When Dawson said something to Dole about all of his hard work and late nights, Dole joked, "Aw, I left the light on and went home."

Dole plunged into local activities, attending 4-H fairs and meetings of the Masons, the Elks, and other social groups. He became chairman of the county Red Cross and taught a Sunday school class at the local Methodist church.

During this period, he and Phyllis decided to start a family. The months passed and they began to consider adopting a baby; they filled out lengthy forms for the Kansas Children's Service League. Only a home study (a visit to the child's prospective home by service officials to look over the living situation) remained when Phyllis became pregnant. The Doles' daughter, Robin, was born on October 18, 1954.

Dole flourished as county attorney. He was reelected in 1954 and again in 1956 and 1958. In the 1956 election he defeated Clifford Holland, Jr., the brother of his first opponent, George. Dole's light continued to burn past midnight.

Dole worked as county attorney from 1953 to 1960 in the Russell County Courthouse. He had been given additional impetus to succeed when his wife, Phyllis, gave birth to their daughter, Robin, on October 18, 1954.

Dole decided to run for national office with a bid for the U.S. House of Representatives in 1960. He is seen here with his traveling companions, Dolls for Dole. The Bobolinks, a singing quartet, are the four women wearing Bob Dole hats; Dole's daughter, Robin, is the second little girl on his left. Phyllis and Bina Dole sewed the campaign outfits.

Late one night, the office light attracted the attention of a man named Huck Boyd, who was en route to Phillipsburg, in northwest Kansas. Thinking there might be a break-in, Boyd stopped his car and walked up the stairs to investigate. He discovered Dole hard at work at his desk. This so impressed Boyd, who was the Republican National Committeeman for the state of Kansas, that he never forgot it. In fact, Boyd spread the word about Dole among important Republicans in the state. He believed the hardworking Dole was someone to watch as a future Republican candidate in national politics.

When Wint Smith, the Republican U.S. congressman from the state's Sixth District, confided to Boyd that he would not be running for reelection in 1960, Boyd suggested Dole as a possible candidate. Smith, a fervent conservative, had served in the U.S. House of Representatives since 1946. The political climate that ushered him into office had changed, however, and Smith had managed to ride out his differences with the less conservative postwar politicians. In 1952, Robert A. Taft and Dwight Eisenhower had run against each other in the Republican presidential primary. Smith, however, had worn a campaign button reading "MacArthur" that showed his preference for the renowned World War II general, even though Douglas MacArthur was not running for office. In 1958, Smith had won the Republican nomination for his congressional seat by a narrow margin of 51 votes. His challenger, Keith G. Sebelius, almost won the nomination, and Smith concluded that his support was dwindling. He decided not to run for office in 1960.

Dole had actively promoted Smith in the tight 1958 contest, so he had Smith's attention as well as Boyd's. Dole's friend from the Percy Jones Army Medical Center, Phil Hart, who had become a U.S. senator from Michigan, had also urged him to seek national office. Everything fell into place for Dole politically. Boyd arranged for him to make a special trip to visit Dane Hansen, who acted as a Republican power broker statewide in Kansas. Hansen had been a great champion of Wint Smith's. Dole's former support of Smith was certainly a positive factor in securing Hansen's backing. Dole made a middle-of-the-night visit to Hansen, who lived 100 miles away. Hansen's unusual schedule did not deter Dole; Hansen himself worked from sundown to sunup. Dole won Hansen's approval in just one visit. The tires on Dole's car helped set a good impression, and Hansen later quipped, "Hell, I knew he was a fiscal conservative. The tires on his car were threadbare."

President Dwight D. Eisenhower makes a campaign appearance during Dole's run for Congress in 1960. About his hero Eisenhower, who was raised in Abilene, Kansas, and later became supreme commander of the Allied Expeditionary Force in Europe during World War II, Dole later said, "Anyone who could work harmoniously with Bernard Law Montgomery, George Patton and Charles de Gaulle had to be some kind of genius."

6

Up the Ladder

IN 1960, DOLE STARTED his first campaign for national office with a flourish that no one had expected. A rather sedate, predictable political gathering honoring Kansas Day was being held at the Jayhawk Hotel, right in the center of Topeka. Suddenly, Dole burst into the lobby, accompanied by a singing quartet called the Bobolinks, a football player riding a tricycle, and a cortege that carried in a mock coffin containing Frankenstein's monster who held a banner reading "You Have Nothing to Fear with Dole." Needless to say, Dole's spectacular entrance captured everyone's attention.

The party regulars looked on in amazement—*now* they had something to fear. Bob Dole commanded attention; he was going to fight for the Republican nomination to the U.S. House of Representatives, and fight he did. A smaller version of the Conestoga wagon, the covered wagon that settlers had used to journey westward across Kansas in the 1800s, was carted from town to town across the state festooned with a banner proclaiming "Roll with Dole." From Russell to Ellsworth, from Colby to Hoxie, the "Roll with Dole" motto appeared everywhere. Dole's wife, Phyllis, sewed colorful outfits for young female supporters known as the "Dolls for Dole." Some wore sombreros emblazoned with Dole's name in capital letters that encircled the brim. Dole could hardly be accused of holding back now. He went all out in his first national congressional campaign.

In some ways he had no choice. One of the other candidates in the Republican primary, Phillip J. Doyle, had a surname voters could easily confuse with Dole's. In an effort to differentiate himself from Doyle, Dole hit upon the crafty strategy of handing out cups of Dole pineapple juice to voters. His campaign workers passed out gallons of the beverage, while Dole sought out the crowd or even the lone voter and spoke a few words to as many people as he could. He prefaced his request for support by saying, "Hi, I'm Bob Dole, like the pineapple juice." When the supply of Dole pineapple juice ran out, loyal campaign workers replaced it with the Libby brand, rinsing out the Dole cans and pouring in Libby's.

The Doles' basement functioned as Bob's campaign office. Workers amplified Dole's tireless 40,000 miles of campaigning by phoning undecided voters or by constructing hand-lettered signs that would be tacked up over as much territory as possible. One of the most progressive campaign innovations of that year was the use of color in campaign handouts—a patriotic red and blue for Dole.

Dole took out a mortgage on his family home to help fund some fledgling television ads; the whole campaign cost $20,000. What he lacked in funds, Dole made up with his drive and the dedication and loyalty of his staff.

Besides Doyle, Dole also had another opponent to contend with—Keith Sebelius, a well-known and well-liked attorney. Sebelius had almost defeated Wint Smith in the 1958 primary. During the 1960 campaign, Keith Sebelius's widowed mother received an anonymous letter, postmarked in Washington State, that accused her son of being an alcoholic. Mrs. Sebelius held strong antidrinking views; she was a lifetime member of the Women's Christian Temperance Union, whose primary purpose was to get people to stop drinking liquor. The anonymous accusation stung Kansas residents to the quick. After all, Carry Nation, the country's leading agitator on behalf of temperance in the early 1900s, had gotten her start in Kansas.

Rumors circulated about Sebelius and also about who the author of the letter might be. Additional letters making the same charge had been sent to officials and others in power. Many suspected someone in the Dole campaign as the culprit, but Dole denied that he or his supporters had anything to do with the maligning letter. The person responsible for writing the letter was never identified.

Dole eventually won the Republican primary. He buried Doyle, who received only 4,423 votes compared to his 16,033. Sebelius came in second, just 982 votes behind Dole. In conceding to Dole, Sebelius explained that the reason for his loss was, "You drowned me in pineapple juice." Dole offered a more serious assessment of the congressional race years later by saying, "I guess I was very competitive anyway and even after the disability I was more competitive. I was trying to prove to myself that I could still make it, still do it."

Dole followed his primary win with an adroit victory over his Democratic rival, William A. Davis. Swept along by the Kansas Republican wave, which had carried a greater percentage of votes for Richard M. Nixon for president than any other state except Nebraska, Dole won his election. Nixon, however, lost the presidential election to Democrat John F. Kennedy.

Dole became a member of the U.S. House of Representatives, "the first branch of the legislature," in January 1961. As he put it, he was a "very junior member" of the newly formed 87th Congress at a time when seniority

Dole and his father, Doran, proudly pose on the steps of the U.S. Capitol in Washington, D.C., in 1961 after Dole became a member of the 87th Congress from the 6th District of Kansas.

counted for a lot. Although he had finally made it all the way to the nation's capital in Washington, D.C., the seat of power, Dole was preoccupied with the fact that Kansas would be losing one of its six House seats after the state had come up short in the 1960 census. The House is the only elected branch of government that gives every voter an equal voice because each member represents the same number of constituents, or residents in a representative's district. Through apportionment, or distribution of legislative seats, representatives are allocated among the states according to population. In 1929, Congress fixed the number of House seats at 435 and allowed the redistribution of seats among the 50 states by the U.S. Census Bureau after each 10-year census. At a reception during his first visit to the White House, when he and Phyllis met President Kennedy and First Lady Jacqueline Kennedy, Dole joked about this new lack of job security as a representative to Rose Mary McVey, the wife of Kansas congressman Walter McVey, saying, "Live it up while you can, Rose Mary. We're parked in a ten-minute zone."

The GOP's freshmen House members elected 37-year-old Dole its president. He won by only one vote, yet this status drew the attention of Representative Gerald R. Ford of Michigan, who had been a member of Congress since 1949. Ford kept his eye on Dole, and in 1976, as the nation's president, he would ask Dole to be his vice-presidential running mate.

As a U.S. representative, Dole had a number of responsibilities. Because he had a tiny staff, Dole perused every letter that came into the office and answered most of them, scrawling a short note on some in his labored cursive. He also acted as tour guide for visiting constituents. He edited a newsletter that he sent back to Kansas each month, and he called Kansas daily. He also had to take as many trips as possible back to Kansas to try to serve as the direct link between his constituents and the federal government. The government funded only one or two trips home for each congressman per year. Dole surpassed this number by far, often returning to Kansas twice per month, and had to pay for these trips out of his own funds.

In *Unlimited Partners,* Dole recounted one of his visits to a small town in his home state. A local radio station, trying to draw people to the event, produced a humorously garbled introduction of Dole. "The guest at this evening's dinner will be Congressman Bob Doyle [*sic*]. . . . Tickets have been slashed from three dollars to one dollar. . . . Doyle was born in Kansas. . . . He fought in Italy, where he suffered a serious head injury. Then he went into politics."

Dole took his job seriously and never missed a House vote. The House of Representatives has considerable authority because it initiates all bills concerning federal taxes and tariffs and allocates funds to government agencies and public institutions. Through connections, Dole gained a seat on the House Agriculture Committee. Most of the House's business takes place in congressional committees, not in sessions on the floor of the House chamber. In a standing committee, such as Agriculture, the members consider bills within a specific subject area. Other standing committees include Armed Services, Foreign Affairs, Appropriations, and Judiciary. Legislation is developed by the committees for consideration by the full House, which usually respects the decisions and recommendations made by the committees. Committee assignments, therefore, can be the most important factor of a member's success in Congress.

As a member of the House Agriculture Committee, Dole heard rumors concerning scheming businessman Billy Sol Estes. Estes, with the help of some friends in the government, managed a scam in which he bought empty grain elevators and filled them with surplus grain from the government. The federal government, in turn, paid fees to use the elevators. Between 1959 and 1961, this complex and lucrative business brought Estes $8 million from the

Department of Agriculture. Dole was incensed by this bilking of U.S. taxpayers and by Estes's other shady dealings, especially because they hurt the small farmers— Dole's people. Dole's loud clamor for an investigation by the Agriculture committee landed him a front-page headline in the *New York Times.*

Basically, Dole stuck to the hard-line conservative stance of his party. He felt it reflected what his constituents wanted. He voted against President Johnson's (Johnson took office in November 1963, upon the assassination of President Kennedy) Great Society programs, which included several antipoverty initiatives. But when the 1964 Civil Rights Bill and the 1965 Voting Rights Bill came up for passage, Dole explained his "yes" votes for both by replying, "If American conservatism stands for anything, it is the protection of individuals in all their rights, the right to vote being the most basic in any democracy." Opponents of the legislation, which was enacted, believed that voting for the bills constituted a liberal leaning because the acts forbade discrimination based on race, color, religion, national origin, and in the case of employment, sex. The Civil Rights Act, for example, outlawed discrimination in voter registration, barred discrimination in public accommodations, such as hotels and restaurants, and authorized the federal government to sue public facilities and schools that did not integrate their facilities and to cut off funds to state and local programs that practiced discrimination. The Voting Rights Act was passed by Congress in response to African-American demonstrations protesting voting discrimination.

Dole won reelection to the House of Representatives every two years, for a total of four terms, from 1961 to 1969. In 1968, just as he was getting fed up with the entrenched system of seniority in Congress, Frank Carlson, a popular Kansas senator, told Dole that he had decided to retire. Thus he gave Dole a green light to run for his U.S. Senate seat.

Senate Minority Leader Charles Halleck of Indiana (left), Dole, and Representative Charles Hoeven of Iowa (right) congratulate one another after defeating President Kennedy's farm bill to reduce the federal government's $7 billion stockpile of farm surpluses in June 1962. The Republican members of the House defeated the measure because it would have subjected U.S. grain growers to tight production controls.

Representative Dole geared up for this major campaign with his traditional Dole pineapple juice and polished political savvy. For this race, he had to win sufficient votes from the entire state, not just from one congressional district. His first step toward the senate seat was to win the Republican primary. Dole's opponent, former Kansas governor William H. Avery, was his friend. As governor, Avery had imposed a new income tax and had lost his next election. Dole revived the issue of the income tax during the 1968 primary. Under the vertical campaign signs that Avery supporters had posted, Dole supporters tacked up horizontal signs to make the signs read:

A
V
E
R
Y
TAXES

Dole won the Republican primary on August 6, 1968. He also scored an easy win against his Democratic opponent, Wichita lawyer William Robinson. Dole had campaigned throughout Kansas and had won the more populous western side of the state and most of the cities. He had prevailed, along with a new president: Republican Richard M. Nixon.

In 1969, when Dole took office in the Senate, the United States endured great turbulence. The Vietnam War and outspoken opposition to it tore the country apart. College campuses swarmed with student antiwar protestors. President Nixon announced that American and South Vietnamese troops would invade Cambodia, a neighbor of Vietnam's, on April 30, 1970. (President Nixon had started the secret bombing of Cambodia in March 1969 and continued the bombardment until Congress put a stop to it in August 1973.) On May 4, student demonstrations escalated to a crisis point at Ohio's Kent State University when the National Guard fired tear gas and, without warning,

On January 3, 1969, Bob Dole takes the oath of office as a U.S. Senator. Administering the oath are Senate Majority Leader Mike Mansfield (left), Vice President Hubert Humphrey (president of the Senate, holding the Bible), and Senate Minority Leader Everett Dirksen.

shot their rifles into the crowd of students protesting President Nixon's decision. Four students were killed and nine were wounded during the demonstration. U.S. involvement in Vietnam continued to cause great turmoil and division among the American public until the last troops pulled out in 1975.

Dole's respect for President Nixon ran deep. Nixon had campaigned for Dole in Kansas in 1966, but more important, Dole saw Nixon as a fellow survivor: Nixon had triumphed over his own humble beginnings in a California farm town. As a child, he had known hard times—for example, he sometimes had only ketchup to eat for dinner. Dole, too, had endured lean meals as a child.

In 1969–70, Dole fought fiercely for the confirmation of two of Nixon's Supreme Court nominees: Clement Haynesworth and G. Harrold Carswell (the U.S. Constitution gives the Senate sole authority to confirm presidential nominations, including those for the Supreme Court). Neither nominee triumphed over the firestorm of controversy that surrounded their nominations. (Haynesworth was lambasted for his civil rights record; Carswell was accused of being a racist.)

Dole's ferocity in fighting for Nixon's nominees and his partisanship attracted attention in the Senate. When Dole backed Howard Baker of Tennessee for the minority leader's job over Senator Hugh Scott, who eventually won, a fellow Republican, Senator William Saxbe of Ohio, called Dole a "hatchet man" (a malicious critic), adding, "He's so unpopular, he couldn't peddle beer on a troopship." Senator Barry Goldwater of Arizona characterized Dole as "the first fellow we've had around here in a long time who can grab 'em by the hair and haul 'em down the aisle." Some saw Dole's rough partisan loyalty as an advantage. Lyn Nofziger, one of Nixon's speechwriters, quickly perceived Dole as a means through which to broadcast rebukes to those who opposed Nixon. Dole explained in *Unlimited Partners* that "there was a lot of political hardball played in the Senate" back then. Dole had become a master of the game.

On May 4, 1970, the Ohio National Guard fires tear gas and shoots into a crowd of students, killing four of them, at Kent State University. The students had gathered to demonstrate against the Vietnam War after President Nixon announced that U.S. and South Vietnamese troops would invade Cambodia. American involvement in the war in Southeast Asia caused great controversy among the U.S. public until the war ended in 1975.

But not all of Dole's rhetoric sounded the notes of discord. His first speech in the Senate chamber—given on April 14, 1969, the 24th anniversary of his fateful war injury—called for action to upgrade provisions for and treatment of disabled Americans. He began,

Mr. President, my remarks today concern an exceptional group which I joined on another April 14, twenty-four years ago, during World War II.

It is a minority group whose existence affects every person in our society. . . .

It is a group which no one joins by personal choice—a group whose requirements for membership are not based

On June 5, 1970, Republican senator Bob Dole, Democratic senator John Stennis of Mississippi, and Republican senator Edward Gurney of Florida debate "The Senate and the War" on national television. Dole was an ardent supporter of President Nixon and his policies—opponents called Dole "Nixon's Doberman pinscher" or a "hatchet man."

on age, sex, wealth, education, skin color, religious beliefs, political party, power, or prestige.

As a minority, it has always known exclusion—maybe not exclusion from the front of the bus, but perhaps from even climbing aboard it . . . maybe not exclusion from day-to-day life itself, but perhaps from an adequate opportunity to develop and contribute to his or her fullest capacity. . . . Too many handicapped persons lead lives of loneliness and despair; too many feel and too many are cut off from our work-oriented society; too many cannot fill empty hours in a satisfying, constructive manner.

Dole offered specific programs targeted to eight diverse goals, among them increased employment, better health care, and aid to families who have a disabled person as a member.

After having taken the oath as a U.S. senator on his first day in the Senate, he wrote a letter to his daughter, Robin, announcing, "Today is the most important day in my life." Dole's ability to use his own painful experience, translating his hard-earned knowledge into words and action, illustrated just how far Dole had come. In fact, the speech was significant because it marked the first time a member of Congress had identified himself as having a disability. By including himself with others who have physical disabilities, Dole was allowed to discuss certain values, such as dignity, independence, and security, from a personal standpoint. It was these values that he believed should underlie the specific programs he had proposed.

Dole's feelings for the common men and women of the country reached an apex in this April 1969 speech. By identifying himself in the Senate as a fragile, ordinary, and sincere person, he was figuratively taking a lot of people with him into the Senate chamber. From that moment on, Americans with disabilities had a powerful advocate, whose voice would continue to resound in the Senate.

Dole admired President Nixon, who had a background that was similar to his: Nixon had been born and raised in a small California farm town, had known hard times, had served in the navy during World War II, had been elected a U.S. representative and then a U.S. senator, and had climbed to the highest office in the country.

President Gerald Ford (left), Dole's wife, Elizabeth, and Ford's vice-presidential running mate, Dole, wave good-bye to people at the Kansas City airport before departing for Russell on August 20, 1976. Ford and his aides wanted Dole to be "the tough guy" during the 1976 presidential campaign, and they had every confidence that Dole could withstand verbal attacks from the Democrats.

7

"TO BE THE TOUGH GUY"

PRESIDENT RICHARD NIXON dangled one of the most important and powerful partisan positions—chairman of the Republican party—before Dole in January 1971. Partly because Dole believed the job would make it possible for him to rope in certain groups previously ignored by the party, such as veterans, minorities, farmers, and young voters, he agreed to take the position. He also desired the job for a more self-serving reason: The chairman of the Republican National Committee (RNC) wields much power. It is a coveted position in Washington politics because the chairman manages that party's presidential campaign.

Dole had actually been one of several candidates vying for the job when it became available. Dole's chief rival, George Bush, fell out of the running when Nixon appointed him U.S. representative to the United Nations. After Dole expressed his interest in the RNC position, many, including Republican Hugh Scott, opposed him. Dole countered their resistance by encouraging his defenders to write letters of support to the White House, which became flooded with recommendations for Dole. (Although the chairman is elected by the national committee, he or she is actually chosen by the party's presidential candidate at the close of the national presidential convention; incumbent president Nixon would be running for the Republican presidential nomination in 1972.)

After Dole launched a strong attack against the Democrats who criticized Nixon's handling of the Vietnam War (especially Massachusetts senator Ted Kennedy, whom Dole denounced for "the meanest and most offensive sort of political distortion"), on the floor of the Senate, Nixon's attorney general, John Mitchell, told Dole that the job would be his after a meeting of the RNC a few days later. However, instead of a go-ahead, Dole got a call from H. R. Haldeman, Nixon's chief of staff, who, with John

President Nixon (in the foreground), his chief of staff, H. R. Haldeman (right), and an unidentified man walk from the Executive Office Building to the White House in December 1969. After Haldeman called Dole to rescind the offer of the chairmanship of the Republican National Committee—probably because he thought Dole might prove to be too independent— Dole fought back and wrangled his way into the position.

In August 1972, RNC chairman Dole grins as he holds up a $50,000 check for the GOP from Florida governor Reuben Askew of the Governors' Convention Committee Fund. One of the leading tasks the RNC chairman has to undertake is fund-raising for the Republican presidential campaign; the chairman has to "stimulate the party faithful."

Erlichman and Mitchell, was one of the president's closest advisers. Haldeman informed Dole that the offer of the chairmanship had been withdrawn.

Dole had become caught in the middle of some infighting at the White House. He surmised that his White House opponents were worried that he might prove to be too independent of the president and his staff. After much political wrangling, Dole finally won the job as chairman of the Republican National Committee. He named Anne Armstrong of Texas as deputy chairman, the first woman to be appointed to the position.

While chairman of the RNC, Dole increasingly criticized Nixon's enemies. Nixon's special counsel, Chuck Colson, delegated harsh speeches to Dole to deliver on Nixon's behalf. He became the strong, abrasive voice of the Republican party. Dole had gone national now; he had entered the big leagues.

All the work Dole accomplished, however, took a severe toll on his personal life. He had two important jobs that seemed to sustain him more than his marriage. One night Dole told Phyllis, "I want out." He wanted a divorce—it was as simple as that. Phyllis later pointed out

This family portrait of Bob, Phyllis, and Robin was taken in 1968. On January 11, 1972, Bob and Phyllis were granted a divorce on the grounds of incompatibility. Dole later said, "Phyllis and I had been drifting apart. I was caught up in one life, whose demands were escalating, she in another. While Robin was still young she helped keep us together, but it wasn't a happy time for either of us."

that her husband had sat down "for a family dinner only four times during 1971," so she knew there had been a deep rift growing in their marriage; however, she was unprepared for the speed of the breakup. Dole had arranged for an "emergency" divorce, which became official on January 11, 1972. The immediacy of ending their marriage had shocked her because there had been no talk between them about their problems or even about the inevitability of a divorce.

Dole had gone to President Nixon before he filed for a divorce and offered to resign from the RNC. Divorce was not as common in the early 1970s as it is today, especially among elected officials. Dole worried that his divorce might cast a bad light on the RNC. Instead of accepting Dole's resignation, Nixon gave him a book about the British politician Benjamin Disraeli, whose scandalous personal life had clashed with his political success. Nixon wished to emphasize to Dole that he believed the public and private lives of politicians should be judged separately. Dole was reassured by Nixon's support.

Phyllis had always tried to accommodate the rigors of political spousehood with a good grace. After the divorce, she remained a strong supporter of Dole as a politician and sold hand-painted "Dole for President" pins during his 1988 presidential campaign. As parents, Bob and Phyllis continued to hold high the best interests of their daughter, Robin.

Dole had problems not only in his private life in the early 1970s but also in his public one. The Nixon presidency holds a special place in history because of the Watergate scandal. Nixon's own involvement in covering up wrongdoing that had been sanctioned by him and by his aides astounded the American public, who watched the televised Senate hearings on Watergate in record numbers. Never before had politics been so popular.

Like a political soap opera, the events involved obstruction of justice, a list of enemies, illegal wiretaps on newsmen, secret slush funds, and the firing of the government-appointed special prosecutor, Archibald Cox. The revelation by former White House counsel John Dean, on the witness stand, that Nixon had secretly audiotaped meetings in the Oval Office heightened the drama, which eventually led to Nixon's resignation and to Vice President Gerald Ford assuming the presidency.

But before the scandal broke, Nixon's reelection to the presidency loomed. It was Dole who made up the infamous nickname for the Committee to Reelect the President (CRP): CREEP. The word *CREEP* also implied the secrecy of the Watergate burglars' activities, that they had had to creep around to obtain their information.

The RNC and CRP oversaw different aspects of Nixon's campaign in 1972. In June, five men hired by CREEP broke into the offices of the Democratic National Committee, located in the Watergate office complex, to bug the office, steal information, and make work for the Democratic campaign more difficult. The burglars were caught and arrested. Despite the break-in, Nixon, who denied any involvement in it, was reelected president by a landslide victory.

Two weeks after his reelection, Nixon commanded Dole's presence at Camp David, the presidential retreat in the Maryland countryside. Although Dole himself had been thinking of resigning the RNC chairmanship, it came as a blow to him when Nixon asked Dole to travel to New York and sound out George Bush about taking the chairman's job. Such a request galled Dole, but he was loyal and agreed to make the trip. When he met with Bush, Bush was noncommittal. But to his chagrin, Dole learned later that Bush and Nixon had already talked about Bush taking the position before Dole even made the trip, and Bush had agreed to accept the RNC chairmanship. Later, Senator George McGovern of South Dakota, Nixon's Democratic opponent in the 1972 presidential election, would say of this manipulation of Dole by Nixon and his aides, "It always struck me as rather brutal the way they treated him after the election."

By 1974, when the winds of impeachment whispered around Washington, Dole's distance from President Nixon bolstered his own claim of innocence in the scandal. Fortunately for Dole, Nixon's advisers had formed a "human bottleneck" around the president, cutting Dole off from any personal contact with Nixon. He asserted that he had had nothing to do with the Watergate break-in, as Nixon and his advisers might have. (In legal terms, Nixon became an unindicted coconspirator.) Still, the political fallout of Watergate tinged Dole's 1974 reelection campaign for his seat in the Senate. President Nixon resigned in disgrace on

August 8, 1974; Vice President Ford became president. Less than a month later, President Ford pardoned Nixon. The pardon stirred up even more anger and resentment among the American people.

Dole's campaign, burdened by the turbulent political times, ran into serious trouble. His sisters, Norma Jean and Gloria, his mother, Bina, and his daughter, Robin, pitched in to campaign for him. As the back-and-forth publicity heated up, Dole's campaign staff came up with the idea of placing two pictures of him side by side in an ad: one showed Dole facing the viewer, the other showed Dole's disabled right hand. A bold headline ran above the photos, "You can sum up Senator Bob Dole with a 4-letter word: GUTS."

Dole won the election by a small margin of 14,000 votes. In retrospect, he believes that having been rejected by Nixon's advisers might have saved his political life.

Dole's personal life experienced a major upturn. He had begun to date Harvard-educated lawyer Elizabeth Hanford, whom he had met in 1972 after his divorce. Hanford worked as deputy assistant to Virginia Knauer in the Office of Consumer Affairs. Born in Salisbury, North Carolina, in 1936, Hanford had attended Duke University as a political science major and graduated with honors in 1958. In addition to postgraduate work at England's Oxford University, Hanford studied at Harvard, receiving a doctor of laws degree in 1965. In 1973, Hanford became a commissioner of the Federal Trade Commission, an independent regulatory agency that helps to enforce federal antitrust laws, to protect consumers from deceptive marketing practices, and to prevent unfair methods of competition in commerce.

Hanford first met Dole when he was RNC chairman. Virgina Knauer and she had gone to Capitol Hill to ask Dole to include a consumer plank in the Republican party platform at the 1972 national convention. They believed consumer affairs should be formally recognized in the party's platform. Hanford's first impression of Dole when he walked into the meeting was "My! What an attractive man!" Dole related later that he scribbled her name down on his blotter after she left.

Well into their courtship, Hanford took Dole to meet her parents in Salisbury. Dole wanted her parents to know the full extent of his war injury, and early one morning he appeared in the kitchen while Mrs. Hanford was cooking breakfast. Dole had placed a towel over his right shoulder, and he was not wearing his shirt. "Mrs. Hanford, I think you ought to see my problem," he said, as he pulled the towel off to reveal his injured shoulder. "That's not a problem, Bob," she replied. "That's a badge of honor."

Bob and Elizabeth married in the Bethlehem Chapel of Washington Cathedral on December 6, 1975. During the ceremony, Dole did not wait to be asked the traditional question during the exchange of the vows but eagerly blurted out his "I do" at the first pause in the ceremony. The couple then embarked on their honeymoon to the Virgin Islands. Dole's father, Doran, who was staying in Dole's Washington apartment in the Watergate complex before returning to Kansas, had a sudden heart attack the day after the wedding and died. The Doles cut short their honeymoon as soon as they had received the news of Doran's death.

Many of Dole's friends believe that Elizabeth has had a mellowing effect on her husband, yet to those who know Dole well, his sympathy for people who are less fortunate is not all that new. His advocacy for the downtrodden extends back to the compassion he felt during his tenure as Russell County attorney and during his work with abused children. In 1975, while serving on the Senate Select Committee on Nutrition, Dole proposed a radical-sounding amendment, a reorganization of the food stamp program. During the committee's investigation into nutrition programs, he had been upset to learn that people had to apply for and prove their eligibility for food stamps. It often took weeks for a destitute person to have the privilege of paying $100 for $150 worth of food stamps. Dole knew firsthand how desperate farmers could become when they lost a crop.

Dole's radical notion had at its foundation the idea that hungry people needed food right away. He formed a surprising coalition with Senator McGovern, chairman of the Senate Select Committee on Nutrition and Human Needs. In the Dole-McGovern bill, the two senators proposed that there be an income ceiling (people with a certain income

Bob and Elizabeth are seen here at their wedding, which was performed by Senate chaplain Reverend Edward Elson at Washington Cathedral on December 6, 1975. The newlyweds are flanked by Elizabeth's sister, Burnell Hanford, who was matron of honor, and Bob's friend, Assistant Defense Secretary Robert Ellsworth, who was best man.

were not eligible) for people applying for food stamps, but for those whose income fell below this ceiling, food stamps would be free of charge. In fact, Congress ended up doubling the money for food stamps. After conducting hearings all over the country, Congress expanded the school lunch program and began the Special Supplemental Food Program for Women, Infants, and Children (WIC), which provides free food for poor, pregnant, or nursing women and their children.

By 1976, Dole clinched his status as a national figure by accepting the vice-presidential nomination from President Gerald Ford, who was running for president. Although *Newsweek* called Ford's selection of Dole "impulsive" and Dole the "cut-and-shoot junior Senator from Kansas," Ford and his staff believed Dole would shore up Republican support in the heartland and would not be afraid to attack their Democratic opponents or to handle the criticism. Ford told Dole, "You're going to be the tough guy."

Ford and Dole opened their campaign in the heartland of America: Russell, Kansas. The people of Russell had never seen a president in their town before. Dole's speech on the courthouse lawn began, "I am proof that you can be from a small town, without a lot of material advantages . . . and still succeed. . . . If I have had any success, it is because of the people here."

Dole proved as tireless a worker as ever. He flew from engagement to rally to fund-raiser. Relentlessly on the move, he logged 62,000 miles of travel in 44 states over nine weeks. His wife helped, too, later saying, "We went to the same cities, split off on separate agendas and joined up again in the evening." Elizabeth, who had taken a leave of absence from her position at the Federal Trade Commission, tried to cover as much ground as she could to assist her husband's campaign.

Opposing the Ford-Dole ticket were Democrats Jimmy Carter, former governor of Georgia, and Senator Walter

On October 15, 1976, Dole makes a point as Senator Walter Mondale (left) reads his notes in the first nationally televised vice-presidential debate. More than 10 years after the debate, during which Dole dropped the bombshell that the wars of the 20th century were "all Democrat wars," he remarked that the debate had "taught me to think twice before saying something that might appear insensitive or call into question the patriotism of any American."

Mondale of Minnesota. Because television had assumed a wider role in political campaigns than the print media had, public relations people in both parties arranged for the very first nationally televised debate between vice-presidential candidates. Dole began the debate, which was held on October 15 in Houston, Texas, in an amiable mood, citing his friendship with Senator Mondale; however, as the words began to fly, Mondale tried to connect Dole to the Watergate scandal. Dole replied that Watergate was not an issue; then he lashed out with a comment that the Vietnam War, World War II, the Korean War, and World War I were "all Democrat wars . . . all in this century." Dole looked furious when he made this statement and he glowered—on national television.

Mondale retorted, "Senator Dole has richly earned his reputation as a hatchet man tonight," recalling Senator William Saxbe's nickname for Dole. After the debate, Dole did not let up on his campaigning, but his hard work ultimately failed to win the election. Carter and Mondale beat the Ford-Dole ticket by 2 percent of the electoral vote. The day after the election, Dole's state of exhaustion turned into illness. He took to his bed.

But Dole set his sights on a campaign four years ahead, the 1980 race for president. He decided to run for the job himself. Meanwhile, he worked to erase his image as a hatchet man. One of the ways he could accomplish this came naturally: He would continue the work he had started with Senator McGovern. McGovern once described Dole as someone who has a "real compassion for people that need help from the government. The notion he's a hard-edged scrooge just doesn't hold up for the people that really need help."

Dole and his daughter, Robin, kiss his mother, Bina, on Mother's Day, May 13, 1979. Dole announced his candidacy for the presidency in Russell on the following day, which the town celebrated as Robert Dole Day.

Dole teamed up with McGovern to cosponsor a bill that paid farmers the full price for a bushel of wheat but actually paid them not to grow it. This was called a "set aside," and it allowed the land to lie fallow, or uncultivated, so that the soil could regenerate itself for future crops. At the same time, Dole introduced a bill calling for an amendment to balance the federal budget, thereby counteracting any opinions that he was a big spender.

On May 14, 1979, surrounded by his family, Dole announced his candidacy for the presidency in front of Russell's city hall. First he defined the "great task" of "reasserting a common faith in all that we once set out to be as a nation, a shared confidence in those means established to help us grow and prosper in freedom, and a common conviction that we are in truth what we say we are: a nation that hews to the self-evident truth that all men are created equal." He continued to outline a plan and a noncombative campaign.

But his campaign failed. Dole had been caught between his two full-time jobs: active senator and political candidate. He would fly out to campaign after a full day of debate on the Senate floor only to be back debating early the next day. His campaign organization became chaotic, while he maintained an impressive record of voting 95 percent of the time. He finished last in the Iowa caucuses and in the New Hampshire primary, and then he dropped out of the race. He later asserted, "Sometimes I think I never really ran for president in 1980." Former actor and governor of California Ronald Reagan won the nomination and the presidency. Dole considered dropping out of politics altogether. He thought about joining a Washington law firm; however, he realized he enjoyed politics more than practicing law. In January 1981, he took on the chairmanship of the powerful Senate Finance Committee. During the Reagan years, the committee proposed to cut individual income taxes and federal spending. The proposal became law in 1981, when the Economic Recovery Tax Act

(ERTA) was passed by Congress. President Reagan asked Congress to increase the debt limit to nearly $1 trillion; the law also provided a huge reduction in tax rates, with special reductions for business. "Reaganomics" had arrived, an era in which many people saw the tax burden shift from corporations to individuals, from higher-income to lower-income people. One bill President Reagan supported, the Kemp-Roth bill, proposed tax reductions that would translate as an $8,000 gain for the wealthiest 1 million households, while costing 19 million households $390 annually.

In 1981, Elizabeth Dole joined the White House staff as assistant to the president for public liaison. Both Doles had emerged as political luminaries at the center of Washington and they had become America's "power couple." Senator Dole pushed a major bill that eventually became the Tax Equity and Fiscal Responsibility Act (TEFRA) of 1982, which lowered the deficit by almost $100 billion, with most of the savings coming from spending cuts and about 10 percent of the funds coming from new taxes. The bill cut out tax breaks on such activities as travel, while it raised taxes on luxury items such as cigarettes. When it came to a vote in July 1982, the measure passed with the help of a majority of Democrats. The *Washington Post* dubbed Dole the "New Lion" of the Senate. People began to consider him a serious possibility for the 1984 presidency if Reagan decided not to run for reelection.

The power base of the Doles kept growing. President Reagan appointed Elizabeth Dole secretary of transportation in 1983. At Washington's annual Gridiron Dinner that March, she captured the attention of everyone by her response to the final remark in her husband's speech that under no circumstances would Dole run for president in 1984. She quickly stood up, smiled, and quipped, "Speak for yourself, sweetheart."

On April 14, 1983, the anniversary of Dole's war injury, he announced the formation of the Dole Foundation, an organization that focuses on employment for people with disabilities. For example, the foundation has funded New York City's National Theater Workshop for the Handicapped and promoted the employment of mentally retarded workers at fast food restaurants in Kentucky. More than 24 epileptics have been trained for jobs through Ohio's Epilepsy Foundation. In just 12 years of activity, the Dole Foundation has awarded more than $6 million in grants. Dole acts as chairman, signs letters when he can, and appears at fund-raisers for the foundation.

Personal loss hit Dole hard later in 1983. His beloved physician, Dr. Hampar Kelikian, died at age 84. Dole eulogized the doctor on the Senate floor by reading Robert Frost's poem "Nothing Gold Can Stay." In August, Bina Dole suffered a heart attack and then died on September 5. Dole said he would always remember his mother as being an inspiration—a tireless worker who never admitted defeat.

In October 1983, Dole supported legislation making the late Dr. Martin Luther King, Jr.'s, birthday, January 15, a national holiday. In *Unlimited Partners,* Dole wrote, "I'm a conservative Republican, King was a liberal Democrat, but the ideals I defended in the mountains of Italy forty years ago included the rights for which King fought on the streets of Birmingham and Selma." Leading the final debate on the bill, which Congress passed, Dole declared:

Senator Dole checks the name tag of a woman attending a Multiple Sclerosis Society meeting in Washington, D.C. In 1983, the senator from Kansas started the Dole Foundation, an organization that concentrates on finding employment for people with disabilities.

A nation defines itself in many ways; in the promises it makes and the programs it enacts, the dreams it enshrines or the doors it slams shut. . . . Thanks to Dr. King . . . America wrote new laws to strike down old barriers. She built bridges instead of walls. She invited the black man and woman into the mainstream of society—and in doing so, opened the way for women, the disabled, and other minorities who found their own voice in the civil-rights movement.

President Reagan won a second term in office with a landslide victory in 1984, an election that gave Republi-

During a light moment at the White House, President Ronald Reagan (seated) presents his fiscal 1986 budget to Senate Majority Leader Dole and Senate Minority Leader Robert Byrd (behind Reagan), while Vice President George Bush (far left) and chairman of the Senate's Judiciary Committee, Senator Strom Thurmond of South Carolina (right) look on. As majority leader of the Senate, Dole decided which bills came up for debate on the Senate floor and helped steer them through the legislative process.

cans a majority in the Senate. Dole attained one of the highest pinnacles of influence when he became majority leader of the Senate. Former majority leader Robert C. Byrd once commented, "The minority leader speaks for his party. But the majority leader, whether he be a Democrat or a Republican, is the leader of the Senate." Majority leaders technically conduct the business of the Senate; they determine what bills come up for debate, and they help to forge agreements among senators in order to get bills passed into law. A majority leader needs to have a persuasive personality and a resolute will to organize his colleagues and bargain astutely. According to Donald A. Ritchie, a historian of the U.S. Senate, "A leader also needs the political expertise to monitor committees, understand how the contents of bills are decided, and gauge the needs, problems, and personalities of individual senators. And a leader must know Senate rules well enough to steer bills through and to prevent the opposition from using shrewd parliamentary maneuvers to side-track legislation."

Dole moved to the majority leader's prestigious office (down the hall from his former office), which has, he joked, the "second best view" in the city (the White House has the best). The majority leader's office also had an elegant reception room and a ceiling of patriotic frescoes.

In addition to working closely with the Senate, majority leaders must generate public support for certain bills. This involves television and radio interviews, fund-raising activities, and meetings with citizens and government officials. The busy schedule occupied Dole from dawn to late evening most days.

Dole's power base among Republicans in the Senate was secure. When the Republicans lost control of the Senate in 1986 (the midterm elections altered the balance, giving Democrats a majority of 55 seats to the Republicans' 45), Dole became Senate minority leader. (A minority leader requires skills similar to those of the majority leader, although the minority leader's party does not have the votes to carry a bill through the Senate.)

Dole sought the 1988 Republican presidential nomination, guided by his unflagging work and political shrewdness. He announced his candidacy, once again, in Russell and brought the cigar box that had held contributions for the Bob Dole Fund when he had needed financial help before. The town came through for him once again, but his Republican rival, George Bush, won the primary and eventually the election in November.

Dole had to pick himself up from defeat once again. This time he did not consider leaving politics, as he had after his 1980 defeat. He realized it had become his lifeline.

After election day in 1992, Dole pays tribute to former president George Bush and is nearly overwhelmed with emotion after saying that the best man did not win the election (Democrat Bill Clinton won). Although he had been a rival of Dole's in the 1988 Republican primary and went on to win that election, Bush later said of Dole, "My respect for his leadership knows no bounds."

8

"DOLE ISN'T BEING DOLE"

DOLE'S RESILIENCE WAS PUT TO THE TEST during George Bush's presidency. Bush's assessment of Dole's allegiance offered high praise: "After I got the nomination, the scar tissue was still there, but Bob is a thoroughgoing pro, and he went right to work to support the ticket. Once I became president, Senator Dole lined up his troops and supported me in every way possible. . . . My respect for his leadership knows no bounds."

A June 1990 article in the *Washington Post* pronounced, "To those who know Dole best, his self-discipline and resilience is no surprise." One of the incidents the *Washington Post* cited was Dole's April meeting in Iraq with that country's president, Saddam Hussein. Hussein talked about the suffering his country had endured during the eight-year Iran-Iraq war. At the end of Hussein's speech, Dole said, " ' I've never spoken personally like this, but do you see this arm?' and he gestured with his withered right arm. 'I have this daily reminder of the futility of war,' he said. Even the Iraqi leader sat in stunned silence." Dole had learned how to use his war injury for what he believed was the highest good. This was no small feat for the former soldier who had long ago endured a horrible vision of himself selling pencils on a street corner.

The year before, the Doles had been sent to visit Armenia after a massive earthquake had killed 30,000 people and rendered 600,000 homeless. Armenia had been the first homeland of Dr. Hampar Kelikian, so seeing the devastation affected Dole deeply. "It's always hard when you see people's faces," he said, in sympathy with the survivors. Dole hung pictures of Armenian children in his office as he fought for a resolution marking the 75th anniversary of the Turkish massacre in 1915–23 of thousands of Armenians with a day of remembrance in the United States. The resolution, however, failed in the Senate.

A very important piece of legislation for Dole was signed into law by President Bush on July 26, 1990: the Americans with Disabilities Act (ADA). The act, which took effect on July 26, 1992, prohibits discrimination in employment, public accommodations, telecommunications, and transportation against people with physical or mental conditions that "substantially limit" a major life activity, such as seeing, walking, speaking, breathing, or learning. The definition of "disabled" includes people with AIDS (acquired immunodeficiency syndrome) and HIV (the virus that causes AIDS) and drug addicts and alcoholics who are undergoing treatment. More than 43 million Americans benefited from the bill, which passed in the Senate by a vote of 91 to 6.

In 1991, Dole acted as the mediator between Republicans and Democrats as they hammered out a new civil rights bill concerning protection of minorities (including people with disabilities) in the workplace. Dole's Senate office hosted the negotiators, who often perused a thesaurus to find words that were acceptable to all parties. Dole brokered some of the major components of the bill, which allowed it to pass. One specific provision he authored

Senate Minority Leader Dole and Senate Majority Leader George Mitchell of Maine (right) attend a meeting on the American economy and environment with President Bush (center) in April 1990. A Senate colleague once said of Dole, "He never gets too high, and he never gets too low.... That's very important, whether you're in the infantry or in the Senate. When everyone else is jumping around, he's very steady."

provided funds for technical assistance in the form of grants the Justice Department makes to local governments for educational seminars on how neighborhoods can meet the requirements for accessibility (by constructing ramps and altering curb corners, for example).

During a conversation with President Bush in the fall of 1991, Dole hinted about the possibility of not running for reelection to the Senate in 1992. Upon hearing this news, President Bush led Dole into a private room and looked him in the eye. "You've got to run again," he said. "I really need your help." Dole decided not to retire and assisted Bush in his legislative agenda.

Dole had other problems that had surfaced in the summer of 1991. He noticed that after going to bed at night he had to get up frequently to go to the bathroom. He went to his doctor, who diagnosed him with prostate cancer. At first he was overwhelmed by the diagnosis; cancer of the prostate gland ranks third among the types of cancer that kill American men. Dole sought all the information available about the cancer. Elizabeth, who had become head of the American Red Cross the year before, helped her husband learn more about the disease. If the disease is detected early, it can be cured. If the cancer has not spread, surgical removal of the prostate gland is recommended by most doctors. Dole opted for surgery in December 1991, and the operation was a success. He decided to publicly disclose his bout with cancer, in spite of the advice he received from others to the contrary.

After the operation and recuperation, Dole appeared on a segment of "Face the Nation," a television program broadcast on the CBS network, and gave his own advice to the men in the audience by recommending that they get a PSA (prostate specific antigen) test. A PSA consists of a blood analysis; however, it is not always 100 percent accurate. On March 11, 1992, *People* magazine featured Dole in its Coping section, in which Dole described how he chose to run again for another term. He said it was as difficult a decision to make as whether or not to have prostate surgery because, "you get cut up in either case."

When the next presidential campaign began, George Bush claimed the Republican nomination handily and ran against Democrat Bill Clinton, the governor of Arkansas. Dole jumped into the campaign melee with his harsh, partisan rhetoric, and claimed Clinton was being "disingenuous" (insincere) to the American public about his military draft record. During the Vietnam War, Clinton had obtained a deferment from military service when he went to study at Oxford University. Dole added that Senator Albert Gore of Tennessee, who was Clinton's running mate, had at least been to Vietnam, albeit as a journalist. Clinton's press secretary, Dee Dee Myers, retorted, "Bob Dole is a very straightforward, snarling attack dog when he wants to be." Although he probably felt some bitterness toward Clinton after Clinton won the presidency, Dole did not sound disheartened. "I thought it was time to establish myself as a leader," he later commented.

After Clinton took office in January 1993, the Republicans initiated a filibuster (a parliamentary maneuver used in the Senate by which a minority of senators try to frustrate the will of the majority by literally "talking a bill to death," thereby causing its withdrawal or death) against President Clinton's economic stimulus plan. Clinton's plan called for $16.3 billion to be poured into the American economy, which Dole believed would only add to the federal deficit, especially because the expenditure was not matched by cuts in spending. As minority leader, Dole commanded the Republicans' attack, which eventually stymied the White House plan, and Clinton soon abandoned it. Newt Gingrich, the House minority leader, praised Dole to a reporter of the *Washington Post,* saying, "It's the best spring of Bob Dole's political career. . . . He has done an absolutely outstanding job."

Dole continued to wage political war against President Clinton. He joined with House members in demanding a special counsel to look into a shady land deal that involved the Clintons and their friend James McDougal, who owned a bank that had failed. From there, Dole next tackled the health care reforms proposed by the Clinton administration. In his rebuttal speech to Clinton's 1994 State of the Union Address, Dole pointed to an intricate grid that he said stood for all the new bureaucracies the Clinton health plan would create. Dole has long been a proponent of limiting federal government, "making it smaller and making it less intrusive." Like Clinton's economic stimulus plan, the health care reforms never made it past Congress.

On April 14, 1994, the 25th anniversary of his first Senate speech, Dole called for a National Commission on the Future of Disability to examine and evaluate all the current disability programs. (The previous year, Dole had introduced a bill requiring the State Department to report on worldwide discrimination against people with disabilities.) President Clinton attended a special luncheon Dole

In January 1994, Dole honored former president Richard Nixon with a luncheon to celebrate the 25th anniversary of Nixon's first inauguration. Nixon and Dole remained friends throughout the years, and before Nixon's death in April 1994 he encouraged Dole to run again for the presidency, writing, "After 1994, you will have no one who can defeat you if you run, or can win without you if you decide not to run."

had organized for the afternoon of his anniversary speech. There seemed to be no friction between the two rivals at the event. President Clinton said he had reread Dole's maiden speech, which he termed "one of those magic moments in the history of Congress . . . which reminds us all . . . there's a common chord that unites us when we are all at our best." Both politicians share a dedication to people with disabilities.

Dole and Clinton found themselves together again at former president Richard Nixon's funeral on April 27, 1994. Dole's trusted, longtime friend Bob Ellsworth encouraged Dole to talk at the service about the deep feelings he had about the former president. Dole spoke eloquently, ending with the words, "May God bless Richard Nixon. May God bless the United States." Remembering his former friend, Dole began to cry and brought tears to the eyes of many in the audience.

The midterm elections of 1994 ushered in a Republican majority in both the House and Senate in what appeared to many to be a resounding call for change. Dole once again became majority leader, a quiet counterpart to House Speaker Newt Gingrich, who is considered by most to be extremely outspoken and combative. The GOP's Contract with America, a commitment the Republicans made with the American people during the 1994 campaign, enumerates various provisions such as term limits for lawmakers, tax credits, tax cuts, and cuts in welfare, among others. Reducing the federal deficit is the primary goal of this contract, which became the focus of the 104th Congress's first 100 days.

Dole started early to test the waters for running as the Republican nominee for president in 1996. As he put it in an August 1994 interview with *Time* magazine, "I do a lot of traveling. I've been to California, New Hampshire, Ohio, New Hampshire, Iowa, New Hampshire,"emphasizing the state crucial to carrying the Republican nomination.

On April 27, 1994, Dole delivered an emotional eulogy at former president Nixon's funeral, which was held at the Nixon Library and Birthplace in Yorba Linda, California.

In early 1995, Dole appeared on talk shows and television programs of all sorts, including "This Week with David Brinkley," "Meet the Press," "Murphy Brown," "The Tonight Show with Jay Leno," "The Late Show with David Letterman," and "Larry King Live" to name but a few. Hosts appreciated his rapier wit, as well as his straightforwardness. David Glodt, the executive producer of "This Week with David Brinkley," said of Dole, "He always makes news. You know when Bob Dole is on, there will be a headline the next day."

One dilemma Dole had after deciding to enter the 1996 presidential race was deciding whether he should relinquish the job-in-hand of majority leader, the second most important job in American politics, for a chance at the most important one, which he has failed to capture twice before. Some Republicans muttered during the spring of 1995 that Dole should not run for president while serving as majority leader. Others speculated that a Republican ticket with Dole and General Colin Powell, the former chairman of the Joint Chiefs of Staff, would have a good chance of succeeding, although Powell had not confirmed reports that he would be interested in running. On May 25, however, Powell commented, "I want to keep my options open. I'm going to do something to try to make this an even greater country than it is now. Just keep watching. I'll be out there somewhere."

Dole launched his official Announcement Tour for his candidacy for the presidency on April 10, 1995, during a four-day, 10-state tour that ended in Topeka, Kansas, on April 14, the 50th anniversary of his World War II injury. Michael Kramer of *Time* magazine reported that the strenuous schedule was designed "to prove that at 71 he's still vigorous enough for the job." Dole believed that he ought to be president because "I have the experience . . . I have been tested, and tested and tested in many, many ways," and because "I am not afraid to lead, and I know the way."

Dole, however, had stiff competition. Several Republican colleagues officially declared their candidacy for the presidential nomination, including Senator Phil

In June 1994, Dole commemorated the 50th anniversary of D day in Italy; he is seen here waving to a crowd of American veterans and their families.

Gramm of Texas, former Tennessee governor Lamar Alexander, the conservative commentator Patrick Bucha-
nan, Representative Robert K. Dornan of California,
former State Department official Alan Keyes, and Senator
Richard Lugar of Indiana.

Dole, as the front-runner, attempted to acclimate himself to the rightward leanings of the GOP. Many critics
found Dole's new positions (or "flip-flops," as one reporter called them) hypocritical. For example, in 1985
Dole had protested President Reagan's ambition to revoke
the chief executive order on affirmative action (minority
preference programs) that are meant to counteract job
discrimination. In early 1995, however, he recommended
the repeal of such orders, and he championed the GOP's
anti-immigration stance. In another flip-flop, Dole had
voted for an early version of the Brady bill (named for
President Reagan's press secretary, James Brady, who was
seriously wounded on March 30, 1981, during the attempted assassination of President Reagan by John
Hinckley, Jr.), which called for a five-day waiting period
before the purchase of a handgun to enable local authori-
ties to conduct background checks on prospective buyers.
Dole helped get the 1994 crime bill, which contained the
Brady bill, passed; however, in 1995, he favored discard-
ing the ban on assault weapons, an action that, some
believed, confirmed he was pandering to the gun lobby's
power in GOP primaries. In 1988 while campaigning for
the presidency, he had advocated the government's
"stimulating school systems to improve what goes on in
our classrooms," but he reversed himself in 1995, when he
suggested doing away with four cabinet-level agencies,
including the Department of Education. Also in 1988, as
he often had throughout his career, Dole stated that the
federal budget deficit is the "single greatest threat to a
prosperous and dynamic America." He mentioned cutting
taxes, but when he refused to sign the no-new-tax pledge
at the 1988 New Hampshire primary, he lost the race.

*In January 1995, Dole became
majority leader of the Senate
and Newt Gingrich (right)
became Speaker of the House.
In comparing the two
Republican leaders, one
reporter said that Dole is like
a "kindly elder statesman" next
to Gingrich, who is a political
firebrand and maverick.*

On February 3, 1995, Dole exchanges wisecracks with David Letterman on the "Late Show with David Letterman." Dole made an informal announcement on the television talk show that he would be seeking the 1996 Republican nomination for president.

Then on April 21, 1995, Dole signed a no-new-tax pledge in Washington, D.C. Also in April, he attacked Hollywood, saying that it lacks "family values." Some critics believe that in lambasting Hollywood films, Dole tried to "make political hay" by taking a "moral stand" to further his desire to court the party's far-right wing.

DOLE ISN'T BEING DOLE, AND AIDES CALL IT STRATEGY, read a *New York Times* headline on May 13, 1995. The article goes on to state: "Republicans on Capitol Hill . . . have started wondering whether after three decades in Washington, Mr. Dole . . . has lost his touch, or at least lost touch with his colleagues." But Dole's advisers assert that it is "more important for Mr. Dole to prove his conservative bona fides to next year's primary election voters than to demonstrate to Washington insiders how ably he can run the Senate." The advisers explained further that by "standing firmly to the right, even if he does not get his way . . . [Dole] could satisfy critics who contend that he 'is not seen as being passionate about anything or fighting for anything.'"

Some people, such as *New York Times* reporter Richard L. Berke, believed Dole's advisers' strategy could backfire and undermine a major premise for Dole's candidacy: "that he is a fair-minded leader who can work with both parties to get things done."

Dole's position as majority leader of the Senate provides him with much visibility and he has consistently been able to get things accomplished. (Two previous party leaders, Lyndon Johnson in 1960 and Howard Baker in 1980, lost the presidential nomination while focusing their election-year energies on their duties in the Senate.) On the issues, he is not that different from most Republicans: he supports term limits (if they apply to everyone); he is pro-life and for the death penalty; and he supports block grants so people in local areas can decide how they wish to spend the money to combat crime.

In 1995, Dole also had his share of drubbings. In March, he failed to assemble a two-thirds majority in the Senate for a constitutional amendment that would require a balanced budget. In mid-May, he could not muster the votes needed to carve out a legal reform bill in the Senate that was as extensive as the bill that passed earlier in the House. Also in May, he said he would support legislation that would move the American embassy in Israel from Tel Aviv to Jerusalem, setting off protests by the White House and by Jews who believe the move would delay the ongoing Palestinian peace talks.

On June 22, the GOP leaders of the House and Senate announced a compromise on a plan to balance the federal budget by the year 2002 by cutting nearly $1 trillion in spending. Senate Majority Leader Dole and Speaker Gingrich agreed to cut various income and investment taxes by $245 billion over the next seven years. The leaders also acknowledged that no tax cuts would take effect until the Congressional Budget Office (which provides Congress with basic data and analyses of fiscal issues) verified that spending reductions were actually contributing to a balanced budget. Although both chambers must vote on the new budget proposal, they were expected to approve the measures before the end of the summer. The proposal proved to many in the American public that a majority in Congress is committed to controlling spending on popular government programs. But Dole's tough battle as majority leader continues because he must push his congressional colleagues to "go beyond the principle of saving money and decide exactly who will pay the price and how much they will pay."

Many people sympathized with the risk Dole has taken in being blamed for failure in pushing the Republican agenda through the Senate. Richard F. Fenno, Jr., a professor of political science at the University of Rochester in New York, told Berke in the *New York Times,* "it's nearly impossible what he's trying to do, and it's a miracle he's doing so well. . . . He's pretty steady. But how long can he keep it up?"

Whether or not Dole makes it all the way to the White House, he will remain a senior politician and a man who has come to terms with himself. He told a reporter in February 1995 that he had talked to his wife, Elizabeth, about the possibility of losing again, but he had to give running for president one more try. "I don't give up easily," he said, "you never know when your time is. Maybe it's never."

The rigors and strengths of his childhood upbringing in Russell, the trials, both physical and mental, of his war injury, and the long political career that has led him up to the very pinnacle of American power have all tempered Bob Dole into a stalwart person. Ironically, Dole finds many people surprised by his disability. "Every time I go home, somebody says, 'Well, when did that happen?'" he laughs.

His wisdom came to him the hard way. In *Unlimited Partners,* Dole wrote, "Whether economic or physical, suffering can do one of two things to someone. It can

President Bill Clinton and Senator Bob Dole shake hands at a 1993 event in Washington, D.C. In March 1995, a Republican pollster said, "In mid-1993, [Dole] was seen as being overly partisan, unnecessarily divisive and a dark spirit. . . . He is now seen as being an effective leader and someone who is very stable and secure."

toughen him or it can harden him. It can make him more, or less, sensitive to the needs of those around him. He can say to himself, 'I overcame this, the toughest challenge of my life. And if I did, then everyone else ought to be able to do the same thing.'" Dole explains further that suffering can also help a person form a unique bond with other people who have disabilities, enabling that person to combat "the smug belief that physical wholeness is an accurate gauge of a person's abilities."

In his foreword to *Climbing Back,* the autobiography of disabled mountain climber Mark Wellman, Dole entreats readers to "read about Mark Wellman and then tell someone you know: *Disabled* does not mean *unable*." Dole has proven this statement over and over again.

The best general assessment of Dole comes from his friend Robert Strauss, the former chairman of the Democratic party, who declared, "For all Bob Dole's wonderful qualities, his warts, whatever they are, he's a marvelous story of what this country's all about."

FURTHER READING

Cramer, Richard Ben. *What It Takes: The Way to the White House*. New York: Vintage Books, 1992.

Dole, Bob, and Elizabeth Hanford Dole, with Richard Norton Smith. *The Doles: Unlimited Partners*. New York: Simon & Schuster, 1988.

Hilton, Stanley G. *Bob Dole: American Political Phoenix*. New York: Contemporary Books, 1988.

Morris, Eric. *Circles of Hell: The War in Italy, 1943–1945*. New York: Crown, 1993.

Stockman, David A. *The Triumph of Politics*. New York: Harper and Row, 1986.

Thompson, Jake H. *Bob Dole*. New York: Donald I. Fine, 1994.

Wellman, Mark, and John Flin. *Climbing Back*. Waco, Texas: WRS Publishing, 1992.

CHRONOLOGY

1923   Born Robert Joseph Dole on July 22 in Russell, Kansas

1935   Begins work as a soda jerk at Dawson's Drugstore

1939   Germany invades Poland on September 1; Britain and France declare war against
        Germany on September 3

1941   Graduates from Russell High School in June; enters the University of Kansas in
        Lawrence in the fall; Japan's air force bombs the U.S. naval base at Pearl Harbor,
        Hawaii, on December 7, and the United States declares war on Japan

1942   Enlists in the U.S. Army in December

1943   Dole enters basic training at Camp Barkley in Abilene, Texas, in June; travels to
        Brooklyn, New York, for engineering classes; Allies invade Sicily on July 9

1944   Allies land on the beaches of Normandy, France, on D day, June 6; Paris is liberated
        by Allied troops on August 25

1945   Dole is assigned to Company I, Third Battalion, Eighty-fifth Mountain Regiment,
        part of the Tenth Mountain Division, in Italy as platoon leader in February; in
        March, Dole is awarded a Purple Heart after he is wounded by an exploding
        grenade; on April 14, he is seriously wounded during combat on Hill 913; military
        doctors in Pistoia operate on Dole, who is paralyzed below the neck; he is shipped
        back to United States in a body cast and is admitted to Winter General Army
        Hospital in Topeka, Kansas, in June; doctors remove Dole's right kidney after
        an infection in July; Dole is able to move his legs in September; he is transferred
        to Percy Jones Army Medical Center in Battle Creek, Michigan, in November; the
        doctors find blood clots in Dole's lungs and prescribe the drug dicumarol to thin
        his blood; Dole gets pneumonia and doctors receive permission to treat Dole with
        the experimental drug streptomycin, which helps revive him

1947   Dr. Hampar Kelikian performs a series of operations on Dole's right shoulder and
        arm in Chicago, Illinois; Dole meets occupational therapist Phyllis Holden during
        his recuperation at Percy Jones Hospital

1948   Bob and Phyllis marry in Concord, New Hampshire, on June 12;
        Dole enrolls in the liberal arts program at the University of Arizona
        in Tucson in the fall

1949   Dole transfers to Washburn University in Topeka, Kansas, to study history and law

1950   On the Republican ticket, Dole runs for and wins a seat in the Kansas House of
        Representatives

1952   Graduates from law school at Washburn and wins the election for county attorney of Russell County

1954   The Doles' daughter, Robin, is born on October 18

1960   Dole is elected to U.S. House of Representatives

1961   Dole's Republican colleagues in the House elect him as the president of the freshman members; Dole becomes a member of the House Agriculture Committee; calls for an investigation of Billy Sol Estes and his shady dealings with the Department of Agriculture

1968   After serving four consecutive terms in the U.S. House of Representatives, Dole decides to run for the U.S. Senate; he is elected in November

1969   On April 14, Dole delivers his first speech as a senator and advocates the rights of disabled people; he fights for the confirmation of two of President Nixon's Supreme Court nominees but fails to get either one of the nominees confirmed by the Senate; Senator William Saxbe of Ohio calls Dole a "hatchet man"

1971   Dole is elected chairman of the Republican National Committee (RNC)

1972   Divorces Phyllis; in June, burglars break into the Democratic national headquarters in the Watergate office complex in Washington, D.C.; Dole meets Elizabeth Hanford; he helps get Nixon reelected in a landslide victory

1973   Dole is "fired" as RNC chairman

1974   President Nixon resigns from office on August 8; Vice President Ford becomes president on August 9; President Ford grants a full pardon to former president Nixon on September 8; Dole is reelected to the Senate in November

1975   Dole serves on the Senate Select Committee on Nutrition and Human Needs and proposes a reorganization of the food stamp program; Dole marries Elizabeth Hanford on December 6 in Washington Cathedral; Dole's father, Doran, has a heart attack on December 7 and dies

1976   Dole accepts the Republican nomination for vice president, running with President Gerald Ford; on October 15, the first vice-presidential debate, between Dole and Senator Walter Mondale of Minnesota, is televised nationally; the Ford-Dole ticket is defeated by Democrats Jimmy Carter and Mondale

1979–80   Dole campaigns for the 1980 GOP presidential nomination, but he loses to Ronald Reagan; Dole runs for reelection to his Senate seat and wins in November

1981   He becomes chairman of the Senate Finance Committee in January; helps pass the Economic Recovery Tax Act (ERTA); supports the Kemp-Roth tax reduction bill

1982   Dole pushes the Tax Equity and Fiscal Responsibility Act (TEFRA) through the Senate, lowering the federal deficit by $100 billion

1983   Dole announces the formation of the Dole Foundation on April 14; Dr. Hampar Kelikian dies; Dole's mother, Bina, dies on September 5; in October, Dole supports bill to make Dr. Martin Luther King, Jr.'s birthday (January 15) a national holiday

1984   Dole is elected Senate majority leader

1986   When the Republicans lose control of Senate, Dole becomes minority leader

1987   He launches another bid for 1988 Republican presidential nomination but loses to George Bush

1990   Dole meets Saddam Hussein in Iraq; on July 26, President Bush signs the Americans with Disabilities Act into law

1991   Doctors discover that Dole has prostate cancer and operate on him in December

1992   Dole is reelected to the Senate; serves as Senate minority leader and wages political war against newly elected president Bill Clinton

1994   Calls for a National Commission on the Future of Disability in a speech delivered on the 25th anniversary of his war injury; in November, Republicans win a majority in Congress

1995   Dole becomes Senate majority leader in January; he appears on numerous television talk shows; in April, Dole offically announces his campaign for the 1996 Republican presidential nomination; he favors abolishing the ban on assault weapons; he signs a no-new-tax pledge; attacks Hollywood for making movies that lack "family values" and that are "nightmares of depravity" concerning sex and violence; with Dole's leadership, the Senate passes a proposal to balance the budget by the year 2002

1996   Dole continues his campaign to become president

INDEX

Jacobson, Paul, 25
Jennings, Deveraux, 39
Johnson, Andrew, 19
Johnson, Lyndon, 17, 76, 111
Justice Department, 103

Kansas Children's Service League, 67
Kelikian, Hampar, 58, 61, 97, 102
Kemp-Roth bill, 96
Kennedy, Jacqueline, 74
Kennedy, John F., 18, 73–74
Kennedy, Ted, 84
Kennedy administration, 17
Kent State University, 77
Keyes, Alan, 109
King, Martin Luther, Jr., 97
Korean War, 93
Kuschik, Stanley, 40, 44

Lugar, Richard, 109

McBryar, Arthur, 44–45
McDougal, James, 105
McGovern, George, 88, 91, 94–95
Mahoney, Elmo, 63
Manninen, Ollie, 39
Mitchell, John, 84–85
Mondale, Walter, 92–94
Mussolini, Benito, 48

National Commission on the Future of Disability, 105
Nixon, Richard M., 17–19, 73, 77–78, 83–89, 106

Ostrum, Dean, 64–66
Oxford University, 89, 104

Powell, Colin, 107

Reagan, Ronald, 20–21, 95–97, 109
Republican National Committee (RNC), 68, 83–89
Ritchie, Donald A., 98
Robinson, William, 77
Roosevelt, Franklin Delano, 38, 41–42
Ross, Edmund Gibson, 19

Saxbe, William, 79, 93
Scott, Hugh, 18, 79, 84
Sebelius, Keith G., 69, 72–73
Senate Finance Committee, 16, 95
Senate Select Committee onNutrition and Human Needs, 90–91
Smith, Eric "Doc," 63
Smith, Wint, 69, 72
Special Supplemental Food Program for Women,

Infants, and Children (WIC), 92
Strauss, Robert, 113
Supreme Court, U.S., 17, 78

Taft, Robert A., 69
Tax Equity and Fiscal Responsibility Act (TEFRA), 96
Tenth Mountain Division, 39, 40, 42, 44
Tenure of Office Act, 19

Union Pacific Railroad, 28, 29
University of Arizona, 61
University of Kansas, 35, 50

Vietnam War, 64, 77–78, 84, 93, 104
Voting Rights Act, 76

Washburn University, 61
Watergate scandal, 19, 87–88
Wellman, Mark, 113
Woelk, John, 63, 64
Women's Christian Temperance Union, 73
World War I, 58, 93
World War II, 35, 37–45, 48–49, 64, 69, 80, 93, 108

Yale University, 22

Marcia Wertime is a graduate of Swarthmore College and the Bryn Mawr School of Social Work. She is a social worker and freelance writer and contributes to *Physicians' Travel and Meeting Guide*. Ms. Wertime lives with her family in Haverford, Pennsylvania.

Jerry Lewis is the National Chairman of the Muscular Dystrophy Association (MDA) and host of the MDA Labor Day Telethon. An internationally acclaimed comedian, Lewis began his entertainment career in New York and then performed in a comedy team with singer and actor Dean Martin from 1946 to 1956. Lewis has appeared in many films— including *The Delicate Delinquent, Rock a Bye Baby, The Bellboy, Cinderfella, The Nutty Professor, The Disorderly Orderly,* and *The King of Comedy*—and his comedy performances, such as his 1995 role in the Broadway play *Damn Yankees,* continue to delight audiences around the world.

John Callahan is a nationally syndicated cartoonist and the author of an illustrated autobiography, *Don't Worry, He Won't Get Far on Foot.* He has also produced three cartoon collections: *Do Not Disturb Any Further, Digesting the Child Within,* and *Do What He Says! He's Crazy!!!* He has recently been the subject of feature articles in the *New York Times Magazine,* the *Los Angeles Times Magazine,* and the *Cleveland Plain Dealer,* and has been profiled on "60 Minutes." Callahan resides in Portland, Oregon.